Investment Appraisal for Managers

Graham Mott

Investment Appraisal for Managers

First published 1982 by The Macmillan Press Ltd
by arrangement with Pan Books Ltd

ISBN 0 333 34060 4
Printed and bound in Great Britain by
The Pitman Press, Bath

to Valerie and Kay

Contents

1 What is investment appraisal?

Investment appraisal is concerned with managers' decisions about whether, when and how to spend money on their firms' projects. Such decisions are important ones for the companies involved because often large sums of money are committed in an irreversible decision, with no certain knowledge of the size of future benefits.

Suppose a printing firm is considering buying a binding machine for £10,000 which will reduce labour costs on this activity by £3,000 every year for each of the five years the machine is expected to last. What the management of this firm have to consider – and this is no easy task – is whether a return of £3,000 every year for five years justifies the initial investment of £10,000.

The essence of all investment appraisals is to measure the worthwhileness of proposals to spend money, by comparing the benefits with the costs. If this measurement is done badly, it can hamper a firm's growth and employment prospects for years to come, and may lead to an inability to attract new investors. Financial institutions and individuals provide firms with money in the expectation of a reasonable rate of return. If a firm invests that money in projects which do not yield a reasonable return then investors will be wary of that company in the future.

We measure the worthwhileness of investment proposals by building simple financial models of the expected events. Using the binding machine example above we can set out the expected events as cash inflows or outflows for each year of the machine's life, as in Figure 1.1. These cash flows start at Year 0 which is the beginning of the first year when the project is initiated.

The two main aims of this book are to identify the various items to include in the yearly cash flows and to examine the

Figure 1.1 Financial model of the binding machine project

	£
Year 0	– 10,000
Year 1	+ 3,000
Year 2	+ 3,000
Year 3	+ 3,000
Year 4	+ 3,000
Year 5	+ 3,000
Total profit	+ £5,000

available techniques which say whether the investment is worthwhile or not. Subsequent chapters discuss the techniques in depth and show the build-up of the yearly cash flows allowing for taxation, uncertainty and inflation.

Managers are involved in money-spending decisions either as initiators of projects, or as top management putting the final seal of approval on other managers' plans. For example, functional managers may identify profitable opportunities and direct their staff to investigate them more fully. Other staff may approach a functional manager with their own ideas for new investment. An awareness of the factors influencing the profitability of such investments must help managers channel the firm's resources down more profitable paths.

In many firms it is left to the accountant to pronounce a verdict on the viability of a proposed investment project. This presupposes not only that he is trained in appraisal techniques (which he usually is, of course) but also that he fully understands the marketing, production and human aspects of such proposals. Many arguments favour managers from the whole range of business functions being involved in decision making. If you are a manager, you should be aware of the factors that are relevant to a project's profitability. You need to be able to talk the same language as financial managers and accountants. Most of all, you must be able to identify and generate potentially profitable investments for your firms.

Environmental aspects

When appraising projects, managers have to look at both the internal and external factors affected by their decision. If the proposal is, for example, a diversification away from existing activities, we must first see if it fits the corporate strategy laid down by the board of directors, or whether such investment warrants a change in that strategy. Managers today are much more aware of their social responsibility to employees. How does the proposal under review affect present employment and future promotion prospects?

Looking outside the firm, managers should be aware of their responsibilities to the local community in terms of the environment, pollution and employment opportunities. There are also the 'knock-on' effects of services to be provided locally to the firm or to its employees. Firms also have responsibilities to the nation. They contribute taxes to help finance centrally funded services and their exports or import substitutes help pay for our importation of essential foodstuffs and raw materials. Last but not least we must consider the needs of the customer, without whom the firm would no longer be in business.

All of these internal and external factors may influence investment decisions but these are outside the scope of this book, which primarily concentrates on the financial aspects of the decision. This is not to suggest that the financial factors are paramount, but that this book intends that managers should make investment decisions in the full knowledge of the likely financial consequences, not in ignorance of them. We now need to look at the variety of situations which demand the manager's attention and require him to make good decisions.

Types of investment situation

There are a number of basic situations where an appraisal method assists a manager to make a sound decision. These include the following:

1 Expansion – assessing the worthwhileness of expanding existing product lines requiring additional investment in buildings, plant, stocks, debtors, etc.

2 New product/diversification – assessing the viability of the more risky investment in totally new products.

3 Cost saving – assessing the profitability of a cost saving scheme – for example, when an investment in a new machine automates an existing manual process.

4 Replacement – deciding whether and when to replace an old machine with a new one to save operating costs or reduce wastage.

5 Alternative choice – deciding between alternative investments to achieve the same ends – for example, choosing between two or more machines with different financial characteristics.

6 Financing – comparing the cost of purchasing an asset outright with the alternative cost of leasing.

All the above investment situations have the same common approach. In each case we must decide whether the benefits we get from the initial investment are sufficient to justify the original capital outlay. The next chapter examines the available techniques used to decide whether an investment is worthwhile. Chapters 3 and 4 explain how the yearly cash flows are built up in these investment situations and how the effects of taxation can be incorporated.

There may be some investment situations where no benefits are quantifiable in money terms. For example, the government may require firms to invest in fire detection and alarm systems in all their premises. In this case firms have no choice, and although there will be benefits in employee welfare these are not readily quantifiable in cash terms. Even in this kind of situation an appraisal technique could be used to help us make the choice between competing systems which have different financial characteristics. In the case of the fire detection and alarm system one supplier's equipment may have a higher capital cost but a low maintenance cost over a long life. An alternative supplier's equipment may have a low capital cost but high maintenance costs over a short life. We need to formalize this information to make a rational judgement as Chapter 8 on life cycle costing demonstrates.

Uncertainty

In most industrial investment appraisals there is no certainty that the eventual outcome will be exactly as predicted at the time of the appraisal. For example, only in the case of a 'lease or buy' appraisal may we be certain of the size and duration of the cash flows since these are usually expressed in a fixed price contract. But even in this case we may be uncertain about the effects of inflation which may turn out to be at a higher or lower rate than anticipated and which will affect the *real* cost of the leasing payments.

Unless we go back to managing by the seat of our pants we are faced with this problem of uncertain future cash flows whichever appraisal technique we use. There are some crude methods we can use to minimize the risks involved. These methods include rejecting all projects which do not recover the initial investment in a specified number of years or varying the required rate of return according to how risky we view the project.

More scientific methods can be used on important project appraisals where the capital to be spent is significant given the size of that particular company. Computers have an important contribution to make here when repetitive calculations are involved. One of these more sophisticated methods is to test the *sensitivity* of the return on investment to inaccuracies, or variations, in any one item of the cash flow whilst holding the other items constant.

Another method is to draw a *decision tree* which shows diagrammatically the various stages of a sequential decision process. Alternative courses of action open to the firm are depicted as branches of a tree and are assigned probability factors according to the likelihood of their occurrence. The value of each possible outcome is calculated by multiplying the benefit by its probability. The highest profit (or least cost) tells us which course of action to select. A more thorough analysis of risk and uncertainty and a discussion of techniques to deal with the problem is contained in Chapter 5.

Inflation

There may be a tendency for managers to ignore inflation in investment appraisals because its far-reaching effects seem incapable of quantification in any systematic way. It can, however, be viewed as just another uncertainty on a project and incorporated in risk analysis.

The existence of inflation distorts the value of money itself which means the yearly cash flows expressed in pounds may mix chalk with cheese. We need to distinguish between the *real* return on a project and its *nominal* or apparent return. If we receive £100 annual interest on a £1,000 bank deposit our rate of return is 10%. This represents a real return if inflation is non-existent, but if inflation is also 10% our real return is nil. In this case all the interest is used to keep the capital intact although we have received an apparent or nominal rate of return of 10%.

Managers must bear in mind this difference between real and nominal returns when appraising projects. We need to clarify which value of money should be used in the yearly cash flows. We must also decide whether the firm's required rate of return is to be expressed in real or nominal terms. Most firms work in nominal terms and these matters are explored more fully later on. Chapter 6 deals with the effects of inflation on the yearly cash flows and discusses the relationship between real and nominal rates of return. The way in which inflation affects the cost of capital and the minimum required return is reserved for the following Chapter 7.

How much should a project earn?

Firms need to obtain capital for a number of reasons. They need money to buy or extend buildings, to acquire additional or replacement plant, and to increase the amount of working capital tied up in stocks and customers' debts. These items are called assets and are shown in the company financial statement – called a balance sheet – which lists all assets and the sources of capital with which they were bought. Figure 1.2 shows these typical assets on the right hand list and the normal sources of capital on the left:

Figure 1.2 Typical company balance sheet

Sources of capital (a list of the different sources of capital used to buy the assets) Share capital Retained profit Loans, debentures, mortgages, etc.	*Assets* (a list of possessions owned by the firm at the balance sheet date) *Fixed assets* Buildings, plant and machinery, vehicles, equipment and furniture *Working capital* Stocks, customers debts and cash *Less*: Credit from suppliers
TOTAL £ X	TOTAL £ X

If capital had no cost, most firms would be inundated with proposals to spend it on one project or another. It is not free because the providers of that capital expect a return from the company for the use of their capital. The providers of the capital shown on the left hand side of the balance sheet are either the owners of the business or financial institutions reinvesting other people's money.

Owners provide capital in two ways. They provide the company with the original share capital which may be increased every few years by a further issue of shares on a 'rights' issue. In addition, and more significant for ongoing companies, the owners allow the company to retain some of the profit each year rather than pay out all profits as dividends. Whichever form the owner's investment takes, it is only invested in the company in the expectation of a financial reward. This may take the form of income from dividends, or through an increase in the value of the shares.

Occasionally owners may lend capital to their company in addition to providing the company with its permanent share capital and retained profits. It is much more common for financial institutions to perform this role of lending capital to a company. In return they get a fixed rate of interest each year and the eventual repayment of their capital. Institutions performing this function include commercial banks, merchant banks, insurance companies and pension funds. The interest they receive on such investments goes to reward their depositors, policy holders and pensioners respectively.

If we accept that capital is not free then firms are required to earn a rate of return on investments at least equal to the rewards that will satisfy the mix of owners and institutions. No project should voluntarily be undertaken that does not meet this required rate of return unless there are overriding non-financial factors to consider. Some firms express the required rate of return as the current cost of short-term borrowing on an overdraft. This has the merit of great simplicity but does not take into account the cost of capital from the other important sources. The cost of capital is influenced by the desired mix of capital from the different sources as well as by the cost of each type of capital to be raised. We must also allow for the effects of both taxation and inflation which do not bear equally on the different types of capital. A more thorough discussion of the cost of capital is contained in Chapter 7.

The capital budgeting decision

Because capital is not free, and in most firms is usually scarce, managers have to take great care where they invest. Capital is particularly scarce in inflationary times as so much of the retained profit is committed to financing the increased money cost of working capital. Even a constant volume of trade each year requires a firm to find more capital to finance the higher costs of stocks and debtors and to replace old plant at up-to-date prices. This is a case where some firms borrow more to stand still.

Leaving aside the effects of inflation until Chapter 6, firms still usually have more investment plans than available capital. These plans can be categorized into groups. The diagram below in Figure 1.3 shows on the left hand side the different types of capital and other funds contributing to a common pool. The various categories of investments taking up these funds are shown on the right hand side.

Figure 1.3 Annual capital budgeting procedure

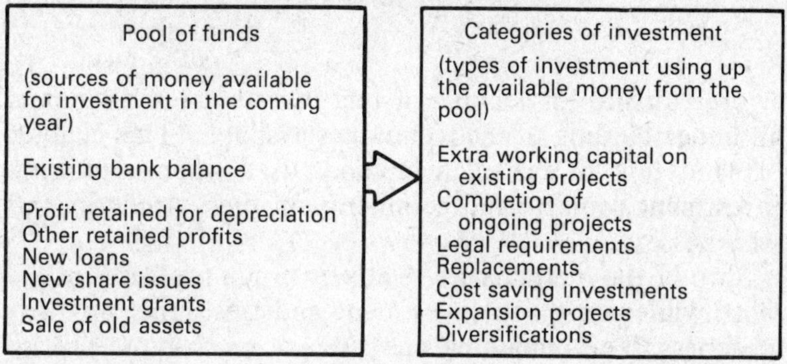

The annual capital budget embodies top management's decision as to what funds will be available for investment in the coming year(s). Such a policy determines the size of the pool of funds which will be used to finance as many investment projects as possible. A capital rationing situation exists when the size of the pool is less than the total investment plans put forward for approval. Firms can either place the investment plans into categories in some order of priority and work through each category in full, or more usually, allocate a proportion of the pool to various categories. When rationing capital either of the above ways we have to consider the consequences of non-fulfilment of any one category against the benefits of fulfilling another category.

Proposed projects often compete in two ways when funds are tight. First they compete against other proposals in the same category and secondly they compete against proposals in all other categories. Whether any one individual project is accepted, deferred or rejected is very much influenced by its profitability or rate of return on investment. The next chapter reviews the main methods used to measure this worthwhileness of an individual project.

2 Which appraisal method should I use?

A prerequisite for looking at real investment situations is an understanding of the techniques available. This chapter explains four of the main methods used when appraising investment projects and comments on their strengths and weaknesses.

Two of the methods are relatively crude measures of the worthwhileness of an investment and this sums up their weakness. The remaining methods are much more precise as they are both based on yearly interest calculations. They are easy techniques to understand and with the help of modern 'hand-held' calculators are not difficult to implement. In recent years more and more firms have been adopting these interest-based methods of appraisal although some firms may retain a payback requirement in addition. Too few managers appreciate that it is only these latter methods that can adequately incorporate taxation, inflation and uncertain future events.

All appraisal methods require an estimate of the yearly cash flows attributable solely to the project under review. These cash flows are discussed in detail in the next chapter but a working knowledge is required at this point to understand the basic techniques which follow.

Typically there will be an initial cash outflow on a project being the cash spent on the physical assets like buildings, plant, vehicles, machinery and the like. If any of these items need replacing before the project ends, then a cash outflow will also occur in that later year. Other cash outflows may occur through the firm building up stocks or giving credit to its customers. These (so called) working capital items will be cash outflows at the beginning of the project or at some subsequent date if increased in amount.

At the end of a project the working capital is released and becomes a cash inflow at that time.

Cash inflows occur, for example, from sales revenue less their wage and material costs. No deduction from such income is made for the use of the assets as their total cost has already been shown as a cash outflow. The accountant's notional charge for the use of these assets is called depreciation. This is not a cash expense but a means of charging a part of the acquisition cost in each year's profit and loss account over the expected life. Where cost saving projects are concerned, the cash inflow each year is the value of these cost savings, again without charging any depreciation. The cost of the investment will be shown in full as a cash outflow at the time of acquisition. It is worth emphasizing at this point that profits which accrue from cost saving investments are just as valuable as profits from investments extending the firm's output.

At this stage all cash flows are expressed in £s of Year 0 purchasing power and inflation is ignored. Chapter 6 describes the impact of inflation on projects and examines the techniques available to cope with it. Many of the other points mentioned so far are elaborated on and illustrated by examples in later chapters but first we need a review of the basic appraisal methods.

1 Payback method

Simplicity is the keynote of this investment appraisal method. Payback measures the number of years it is expected to take to recover the cost of the original investment. It is calculated by estimating the annual cash flows from the commencement of a project to the end of its useful life. Initially the outflow will be negative but within a year or two from the start of most projects the returns or cash inflows will start to flow.

As an illustration let us assume that the board of directors of G. Limited set a maximum period of three years within which any investment must be paid back. They are proposing to invest £200,000 in a machine to save labour costs of £50,000 p.a. The machine is expected to have a useful life of six years. If the point of time when the investment is made is called Year 0, (which is in effect the start of Year 1) then the annual cash flows at each year end can be set out as in Figure 2.1 and the payback period calculated.

Figure 2.1 Calculation of the payback period

Year	*Annual cash flow* £	*Cumulative cash flow* £
0	− 200,000	− 200,000
1	+ 50,000	− 150,000
2	+ 50,000	− 100,000
3	+ 50,000	− 50,000
4	+ 50,000	0
5	+ 50,000	+ 50,000
6	+ 50,000	+ 100,000

Payback period = 4 years.

The apparent simplicity of this method explains its appeal and why firms find it attractive. The example shown in Figure 2.1 was found to have a payback period of four years which could then be compared with the three year criterion set by that particular firm. Whether this approach will always lead to sound investment decisions can perhaps best be examined with the help of another example comparing one project with another.

If a firm relied solely on quickness of payback then in Figure 2.2 Project B would be the one selected. The weaknesses of this appraisal method soon show when the two projects are examined more closely. Although payback is completed more quickly on Project B at $3^1/_3$ years this is very close to the end of its four year life, whereas Project A goes on for two more years. One disadvantage of this method is that cash received after payback is completed is totally ignored. Another disadvantage is that no attempt is made to relate the cash earned on the investment to the amount actually invested. It may be that Project A is more profitable than Project B when looked at over its total life.

Figure 2.2 Comparison of two projects by the packback method

	Project A		*Project B*	
Year	*Annual cash flow* £	*Cumulative cash flow* £	*Annual cash flow* £	*Cumulative cash flow* £
0	− 200,000	− 200,000	− 200,000	− 200,000
1	+ 50,000	− 150,000	+ 60,000	− 140,000
2	+ 50,000	− 100,000	+ 60,000	− 80,000
3	+ 50,000	− 50,000	+ 60,000	− 20,000
4	+ 50,000	0	+ 60,000	+ 40,000
5	+ 50,000	+ 50,000	—	—
6	+ 50,000	+ 100,000	—	—
Payback period:		4 years		$3^1/_3$ years

It may also be that neither project is profitable enough to persuade this firm to invest in them. The payback method does not attempt to measure this total profitability over the whole life of the investment and other methods have to be introduced to do this. However, payback is still used and can yield useful information as an indicator of risk, but is best used in conjunction with other methods.

2 Rate of return method

The rate of return used to be the main method of investment appraisal as it purports to measure exactly what is required, namely, the annual profit as a percentage of the capital invested.

An average profit is calculated by taking the total profits earned on the investment over the whole of its life and dividing by the expected life of the project in years. Profit in this context is after charging the total cost of the investment or wholly depreciating it in accountants' terminology. This total profit is more easily understood as the total cash inflows less the total cash outflows. The average investment is normally regarded as half the original investment on the grounds that it will be wholly depreciated by the end of its useful life.

Figure 2.3 shows the calculation of the rate of return for three projects taking the average annual profit as a percentage of the average amount of the investment.

Figure 2.3 Calculation of the rate of return

Year	*Project A Annual cash flow* £		*Project B Annual cash flow* £		*Project C Annual cash flow* £	
0		− 200,000		− 240,000		− 240,000
1	+ 50,000		+ 100,000		+ 70,000	
2	+ 50,000		+ 90,000		+ 80,000	
3	+ 50,000		+ 80,000		+ 90,000	
4	+ 50,000		+ 70,000	+ 340,000	+ 100,000	+ 340,000
5	+ 50,000		—		—	
6	+ 40,000	+ 290,000	—		—	
Total profit		+ 90,000		+ 100,000		+ 100,000
Average profit p.a.	£15,000		£25,000		£25,000	
Average investment	£100,000		£120,000		£120,000	
Rate of return	15% p.a.		21% p.a.		21% p.a.	

At first glance the rates of return on the three projects in Figure 2.3 might suggest that Project A ranks inferior to the other two projects because the 15% rate is lower than the 21% rate. As the 15% applies for six years whereas the 21% rate applies for only four years some further analysis will be needed before such a conclusion can be drawn. The rate of return method does not readily rank projects in their order of merit.

Turning to Projects B and C it may initially appear that a manager will be indifferent between them as they have an identical rate of return of 21%. A closer look at the timing of the cash flows shows that Project B has some superior claims over Project C. This is because cash is earned earlier on Project B and can be used to repay borrowings or be reinvested. The rate of return method does not take this timing into account in the calculations. It concentrates solely on averaging the total profits earned over the whole life of the project irrespective of the years in which they are earned.

At a later stage it will become apparent that the average investment is a statistical illusion. One reason is that the cost of the investment is often quickly reduced by the early receipt of tax allowances and, possibly, regional developments grants. If these benefits are averaged out over the life of the investment they will not be shown at their true worth to the firm.

True rate of return

The profitability of an investment should be measured by the size of the profit earned on the capital invested. This is what the rate of return method attempts to do without perfect success. An ideal method will not rely on averages but will relate these two factors of profit and capital employed to each other in every individual year of the investment's life.

A useful analogy can be made with a building society mortgage. In this situation the borrower pays to the society a sum of money each year. Part of this sum is taken as interest to service the capital outstanding, leaving the remainder as a capital repayment to reduce the capital balance. The profitability of the investment from the society's viewpoint can be measured by the rate of the interest payment, assuming that the yearly capital repayments have paid off all the mortgage.

Figure 2.4 sets out the yearly cash flows of a typical building society mortgage of £20,000 repayable over ten years with interest at 12% per annum on the reducing balance. The small surplus remaining at the end of ten years is negligible given the size of the annual cash flows.

Present value

The calculations involved in proving the building society's return on investment to be 12% are somewhat laborious. A simpler method is used in practice based on the principles of compound interest. Suppose £1 was invested one year

Figure 2.4 £20,000 mortgage at 12% p.a. repayable over 10 years

	Annual cash flow £	Interest payment at 12% p.a. £	Capital repayment £	Capital balance outstanding £
Year 0	− 20,000			20,000
1	+ 3,540	2,400	1,140	18,860
2	+ 3,540	2,263	1,277	17,583
3	+ 3,540	2,110	1,430	16,153
4	+ 3,540	1,938	1,602	14,551
5	+ 3,540	1,746	1,794	12,757
6	+ 3,540	1,531	2,009	10,748
7	+ 3,540	1,290	2,250	8,498
8	+ 3,540	1,020	2,520	5,978
9	+ 3,540	717	2,823	3,155
10	+ 3,540	379	3,161	6 (surplus)

This building society is getting a true return of 12% p.a. on the reducing capital balance of the mortgage.

ago at interest of 10% per annum. After one year the sum has grown to £1.10. If the £1 was invested two years ago it would have grown to £1.21 with the first year's interest reinvested.

The following is an extract from a compound interest table:

Figure 2.5 The future value of £1 at compound interest of 10%

	£
Year 0 (now)	1.000
1	1.100
2	1.210
3	1.331
4	1.464

Compound interest measures the *future value* of money invested sometime in the past. It is equally possible to look at money in the reverse direction, namely, the *present value* of money receivable at a future point in time. The present value of a future sum of money is the equivalent sum now that would leave the recipient indifferent between the two amounts. The present value or equivalent sum to £1 receivable in one year's time is that amount which if invested for one year would accumulate to £1 in one year's time. Using a 10% rate of interest, £1 receivable in one year's time has an equivalent value now of £0.909 because £0.909 invested for one year at 10% will accumulate to £1.

The following is an extract from the present value table shown in Appendix A compared with the compound interest factors at the same rate of interest:

Figure 2.6

	Present value of £1 receivable in a future year with interest at 10%	*Future value of £1 with compound interest at 10%*
Year 0 (now)	1.000	1.000
1	.909	1.100
2	.826	1.210
3	.751	1.331
4	.683	1.464

The relationship between the factors is that one is the reciprocal of the other for the same year. For example, for Year 4 $\frac{1}{.683} =$ 1.464.

Returning to the building society mortgage illustrated in Figure 2.4 this was shown to have a true rate of profitability of 12%. This can now be proved using the simpler present value approach as in Figure 2.7. To do this the cash flows are tabulated yearly and brought back (discounted) to their present value by the use of present value factors. In effect, interest is deducted for the waiting time involved. The remaining cash is therefore available to repay the original investment. The profitability of the investment is measured by the maximum rate of interest which can be deducted, whilst leaving just enough cash to repay the investment. This rate of interest is the same 12% as found in Figure 2.4. The surplus of £3 is negligible given the size of the annual cash flows.

Figure 2.7 Calculation of the rate of profitability of a £20,000 mortgage repayable over 10 years with interest at 12% p.a. using present value factors

	Annual cash flow £	Present value factors at 12%	Present value £	
Year 0	− 20,000	1.000		− 20,000
1	+ 3,540	.893	+ 3,161	
2	+ 3,540	.797	+ 2,821	
3	+ 3,540	.712	+ 2,520	
4	+ 3,540	.636	+ 2,251	
5	+ 3,540	.567	+ 2,007	
6	+ 3,540	.507	+ 1,795	
7	+ 3,540	.452	+ 1,600	
8	+ 3,540	.404	+ 1,430	
9	+ 3,540	.361	+ 1,278	
10	+ 3,540	.322	+ 1,140	+ 20,003
				+ £3

The rate of profitability on this investment is 12%.

The effect of using present value (PV) factors on the future cash flows is to take compound interest off for the waiting time involved. If a *higher* rate of interest than 12% was applied in Figure 2.7 then not all the capital would be repaid over the ten year life. If a *lower* rate of interest than 12% was used, the capital repayments would be larger each year as the present values would be larger. This would result in the mortgage being repaid in less than the ten years stipulated.

Both the methods of calculation explained above in Figure 2.4 and 2.7 arrive at the same conclusion, although at first sight they may not appear related. That they are related can be seen by comparing the capital repayments in Figure 2.4 with the inverted present values in Figure 2.7 which are almost identical apart from rounding off differences. This will always be the case in examples with constant annual cash flows. The present value approach will also give correct results with any fluctuating pattern of annual cash flows.

3 Net present value method

Managers in industry can use this present value approach to assess the profitability of their investment projects. For example, the directors of E. Limited are considering investing £150,000 on a press to make and sell an industrial fastener. Profits before charging depreciation (i.e. cash inflows) are expected to be £60,000 for each of the first four years tapering off to £40,000 in Year 5 and only £20,000 in Year 6. At this time the press will be scrapped. E. Limited normally require a minimum rate of return of 20%.

The cash flows can be set out and multiplied by the present value factors at 20% to demonstrate whether this project meets the 20% required rate as follows:

Figure 2.8 Calculation of the net present value at 20%

	Annual cash flow £	*PV factors @ 20%*		*PV* £
Year 0	− 150,000	1.000		− 150,000
1	+ 60,000	.833	+ 49,980	
2	+ 60,000	.694	+ 41,640	
3	+ 60,000	.579	+ 34,740	
4	+ 60,000	.482	+ 28,920	
5	+ 40,000	.402	+ 16,080	
6	+ 20,000	.335	+ 6,700	+ 178,060
			NPV	+ £28,060

The net present value (NPV) surplus of £28,060 means that the rate of return is more than the 20% rate of interest used. This is because the annual cash flows are big enough to allow more interest to be deducted and still repay the original investment.

The word *net* in net present value means the sum of the

negative and positive present values and this method of investment appraisal is widely known as the net present value method or NPV method for short.

4 Discounted cash flow yield method

The NPV method answers the question of a projects viability when tested against the required rate of return of that particular company. This required rate is alternatively referred to as the criterion rate, or cut-off rate, being 20% in the above example for E. Limited. Sometimes managers want to know not just whether a project is viable, but what rate of return they can expect on a project. To answer this question the NPV method is taken a stage further. The annual cash flows in E. Limited are discounted again at a higher trial rate of interest. Such trial is an educated guess but a higher rather than a lower rate is chosen because of the NPV surplus which previously occurred.

Assuming a trial rate of 30% was chosen then the annual cash flows can be discounted by the present value factors at 30% as follows:

Figure 2.9 Calculation of the net present value at 30%

	Annual cash flow £	*PV factors* *@ 30%*		*PV* £
Year 0	− 150,000	1.000		− 150,000
1	+ 60,000	.769	+ 46,140	
2	+ 60,000	.592	+ 35,520	
3	+ 60,000	.455	+ 27,300	
4	+ 60,000	.350	+ 21,000	
5	+ 40,000	.269	+ 10,760	
6	+ 20,000	.207	+ 4,140	+ 144,860
			NPV	− £5,140

As there is a deficit net present value of £5,140 the rate of return is less than 30%. This is because too much interest has been deducted to allow all the capital to be repaid. If instead of going to an estimated trial rate of 30% the annual cash flows had been repeatedly discounted at 1% intervals from the 20% required rate then the net present values would have read as follows:

Figure 2.10 Net present values at increasing rates of interest

Rate of interest	*Net present value*
	£
20%	+ 28,060
21%	+ 24,220
22%	+ 20,500
23%	+ 16,860
24%	+ 13,440
25%	+ 10,080
26%	+ 6,860
27%	+ 3,620
28%	+ 640
29%	− 2,280
30%	− 5,140

This shows that before the 30% interest rate was reached a net present value of approximately zero was found at the 28% rate of interest. This is the true rate of return on the project and is known as the *discounted cash flow yield*. In other words the DCF yield is the solution rate of interest which when used to discount annual cash flows on a project gives a NPV of zero.

Interpolation

It would be a tedious task to adopt the above method of successive discounting at 1% intervals but fortunately this is not required. The NPV calculations at 20% and 30% yielded a surplus of £28,060 and a deficit of £5,140 respectively. This provides sufficient information to estimate the DCF yield reasonably accurately by interpolation, which can then be proved by calculation. The interpolation shows:

$$20\% + \left(\frac{28{,}060}{28{,}060 + 5{,}140} \times (30\% - 20\%) \right) = 28.5\%.$$

Another interpolation method takes the form of a simple graph with the rate of interest on the vertical axis and the net present value on the horizontal axis as shown in Figure 2.11 below. The NPVs from the trial at the company's required rate and the further guesstimate are then plotted against their respective interest rates and the two plots joined by a straight line. The DCF yield is where the straight line intersects the vertical axis at a zero NPV.

Figure 2.11 Graphical interpolation to find the DCF yield

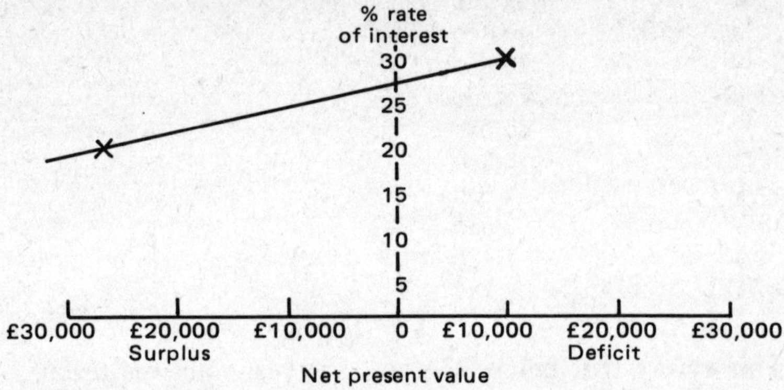

The DCF yield is approximately 28%.

If the two plots are far removed from the actual rate of return the interpolation may not be quite accurate and it should be proved by a final calculation as in Figure 2.12. It may seem surprising that the relationship between the two plots is approximately linear. This could easily be demonstrated by plotting the intermediate NPVs on Figure 2.11.

The DCF yield is 28% as the surplus of £640 is negligible given the size of the cash flows.

It is possible to calculate the DCF yield to one or more decimal places. Although one decimal place may be justifiable there is usually no case for further precision. This is because the basic data on which the calculations are performed are only estimates of future events. To calculate the DCF yield to, say, three decimal places, gives an impression of precision which is illusory.

Figure 2.12 Calculation to prove that the DCF yield is 28%

	Annual cash flow £	*PV value factors @ 28%*		*PV* £
Year 0	− 150,000	1.000		− 150,000
1	+ 60,000	.781	+ 46,860	
2	+ 60,000	.610	+ 36,600	
3	+ 60,000	.477	+ 28,620	
4	+ 60,000	.373	+ 22,380	
5	+ 40,000	.291	+ 11,640	
6	+ 20,000	.227	+ 4,540	+ 150,640
			NPV	+ £640

Other short cuts

The interpolation techniques described earlier are obvious short cuts in the search for the solution rate of interest. Some managers may have access to calculators or computers which can rapidly answer the question of a project's rate of profitability.

Another short cut is applicable where there is a *constant* annual cash flow in every year of a project's life. This method is based on the principle that if a constant cash flow is multiplied by individual PV factors the total present value will be the same as if the constant annual cash flow had been multiplied by the sum of the individual PV factors. This is demonstrated below in Figure 2.13:

Figure 2.13 (A) *Calculation of the NPV using individual PV factors*

	Annual cash flow £	*Individual PV factors @ 25%*	*PV* £
Year 1	+ 60,000	0.800	+ 48,000
2	+ 60,000	0.640	+ 38,400
3	+ 60,000	0.512	+ 30,720
		1.952	+ £117,120

(B) *Calculation of the NPV using a cumulative PV factor*

Years	*Annual cash flow* £	*Cumulative PV factor* @ 25%	*PV* £
1–3	+ 60,000	1.952	+ £117,120

The NPV is identical on both methods of calculation.

If the sum of the individual PV factors (1.952 in the above example) had to be arrived at by literally adding up the individual factors this might be thought to be a long short cut! Fortunately a table exists with all the adding up done for the reader and the total of any number of individual year factors can be read off at a glance. Such a table is shown in full in Appendix B as the present value of £1 receivable *annually* or put more simply a cumulative PV table. An abstract is shown below comparing such cumulative PV factors with the individual PV factors they represent:

Figure 2.14 *Relationship of individual with cumulative PV factors*

	Individual PV factors at 25%	*Cumulative PV factors at 25%*
Year 1	0.800	0.800
2	0.640	1.440
3	0.512	1.952
4	0.410	2.362
5	0.328	2.689

The cumulative PV factors are the sum of the individual PV factors.

The cumulative PV factor table is derived from an independent calculation and may be a 1/1000th different from the cumulation of individual PV factors. This occurs in Year 5 of Figure 2.14. Such rounding errors have little practical significance however, and the cumulation of individual PV factors can be safely used if a cumulative table is unavailable.

Such cumulative PV tables can be used as short cuts to

both the NPV and DCF yield. Because the cumulative table applies only to constant annual cash flows this technique is usually used for rule of thumb calculations on a project's profitability. Very often managers or industrial engineers want a quick guide as to whether it is profitable to pursue a certain course of action. This can easily be done using a cumulative PV table when the cash flows are relatively constant. A more comprehensive evaluation incorporating taxation, grants, working capital changes, etc. can be done later.

Take for example a proposal to introduce a fork lift truck to handle palletized stock in a warehouse at a cost of £50,000. This can be expected to yield an annual saving in labour costs less truck running costs of £18,500. The equipment is expected to last six years and the company regards a 25% return before tax as a minimum requirement.

Figure 2.15 Calculation of the NPV on a fork lift truck project

	Annual cash flow £	*Cumulative PV factor @ 25%*		*PV* £
Year 0	− 50,000	1.000		− 50,000
1–6	+ 18,500	2.951		+ 54,594
			NPV	+ £4,594

The project satisfies the required rate of 25%.

The above method quickly solves the NPV but can be used to even greater effect in finding the DCF yield. Here we require the cumulative PV factor to be first calculated and then looked up on the line of the relevant year of the cumulative PV table, in this case Year 6. Continuing with the fork lift truck example the cumulative PV factor which gives an NPV of zero must be equal to £50,000 ÷ £18,500. This is the cost of the investment divided by the constant annual return which equals 2.703. On the Year 6 line of the cumulative PV table 2.703 almost exactly equates with the cumulative factor of 2.700 at 29% which is therefore the size of the DCF yield.

Comparison of appraisal methods

Four methods of investment appraisal have been discussed so far and useful conclusions can be drawn by comparing these four methods on the same projects. Figure 2.16 sets out three projects with different lives and different patterns of cash flow and appraises them by payback, rate of return, NPV and DCF yield methods.

Figure 2.16 Appraisal methods compared

	Project A	£	*Project B*	£	*Project C*	£
Year 0		− 200,000		− 200,000		− 200,000
1	+ 20,000		+ 80,000		+ 60,000	
2	+ 40,000		+ 60,000		+ 60,000	
3	+ 60,000		+ 60,000		+ 60,000	
4	+ 60,000		+ 40,000	+ 240,000	+ 60,000	
5	+ 60,000		—		+ 40,000	
6	+ 68,000	+ 308,000	—		+ 20,000	+ 300,000
Total profit		+ 108,000		+ 40,000		+ 100,000
Payback period (ranking BCA)		$4\frac{1}{3}$ years		3 years		$3\frac{1}{3}$ years
Rate of return (ranking ACB)		18%		10%		16.7%
NPV @ 12% (ranking CAB)		− £884		− £12,580		+ £15,100
DCF yield (ranking CAB)		12%		8.5%		15%

The payback method selects Project B as the most attractive investment but ignores the short life remaining after payback is completed. This is taken into account however by the DCF yield method which shows up Project B in its true light as the least profitable of all three projects.

The rate of return method selects Project A as the most profitable simply because the average profit per year is more than in the other two projects. When the timing of those profits is taken into account then Project A is shown to give a DCF yield, or true return, of only 12% compared with its rate of return of 18%. Such inaccuracies have persuaded many firms to abandon the rate of return method and use the DCF yield method to appraise projects.

When Project A is compared with Project C on the DCF

yield method the extra £8,000 profit on Project A does not compensate for the slow build up of the project. Even though total profit is £8,000 less on Project C the project is more profitable than Project A because discounting emphasizes the value of the earlier high returns.

In short, payback can yield useful information but must not be used by itself. Either discounting method will give more accurate results than the rate of return method when assessing the profitability of an investment over its whole life. Firms may sometimes calculate the rate of return expected in the first year of operation and compare this with the actual return earned for monitoring purposes. This monitoring or post-audit appraisal is an important part of project investment and is discussed in the concluding chapter. However, the complexities of taxation, grants, working capital and other items reduce the validity of the rate of return method in many cases.

Ranking of projects

There are two ways to rank projects in order of attractiveness. The simplest is to rank them by the size of their DCF yields. When firms use only the NPV method the size of the NPV surplus is not related to the amount of capital invested to earn that surplus. To compare the relative profitability of projects on the NPV method we go a step further and calculate a profitability index by dividing the NPV inflow by the NPV outflow. Taking Project C in Figure 2.16 as an example the NPV inflows totalled £215,100 and the NPV outflow £200,000 giving a profitability index of 1.0755. Any project is viable when the profitability index exceeds 1.000 but its relative profitability against other projects can be measured by the size of the index number. Care must be taken when ranking in the two special situations of capital rationing and the choice between alternative projects. The selection of projects in these cases is discussed in later chapters.

Conclusions

The profitability of investments can best be measured by

a technique which allows for the time value of money. This means the use of either the net present value (NPV) method or the discounted cash flow (DCF) yield method as both are based on interest calculations. Which of these two methods to choose rests solely on the way the question is framed. If management want to know whether a project reaches the minimum target figure the NPV method will answer. On the other hand, if the expected rate of return is required to know how much safety margin exists, then the DCF yield is required.

Both these methods bring each individual year's cash flow into account in the interest calculations without resort to averages. In this way they can adequately reflect the effects of taxation, grants, inflation and other factors that cannot easily be incorporated in payback or the rate of return. Subsequent chapters describe how the yearly cash flows are built up and how we can incorporate these factors in them.

3 What are cash flows?

The inherent nature of any investment decision is the spending of money now in the expectation of getting more money back in the future. No investment is worthwhile that does not recover the original sum invested and provide a reasonable return on the reducing capital outstanding year by year.

Of necessity we must estimate or predict future events, irrespective of the appraisal method used. These future events will be either cash inflows or cash outflows to the business. This chapter is concerned with identifying the different types of cash flows and assessing their yearly value for discounted cash flow appraisal.

Cash flow is a term commonly used by the chairman in his annual report when commenting on the financial affairs of his company. By this he usually means the profit from the trading operations after deducting the tax and dividend payments, but adding back the depreciation charge for the year. It is not difficult to see that cash will be earned by selling goods or services for more than they cost to produce and that some of this cash will go to shareholders and to the tax man. It is not so apparent why depreciation is added back to profit to arrive at the approximate cash flow.

The reason for depreciation being singled out in this way is because it is not a cash expense. All other expenses in a profit and loss account will be paid for in cash either immediately or within the credit period allowed by suppliers. Depreciation is not a cash payment but a notional expense which spreads the cost of an asset, which has already been paid for, over its estimated life. Cash goes out of the business at the time the asset is originally acquired, not when the company charges depreciation as an apportionment of that cost in each year of its use.

Suppose a company invests in plant costing £100,000 which it decides to depreciate at £25,000 p.a. over its four year life. Sales revenue amounts to £200,000 p.a. whilst operating costs amount to £150,000 p.a. If we compare the profit with the cash flow in each of the four years the following figures emerge:

Figure 3.1 Comparison of yearly profit with cash flow

	Profit		*Cash flow*	
Year 0	—		− £100,000	
1	+ £ 25,000	(£200,000 − £150,000 − £25,000)	+ £ 50,000	(£200,000 − £150,000)
2	+ £ 25,000	-do-	+ £ 50,000	-do-
3	+ £ 25,000	-do-	+ £ 50,000	-do-
4	+ £ 25,000	-do-	+ £ 50,000	-do-
Total	+ £100,000		+ £100,000	

In total the profit and cash flow are identical over the project's whole life, but the timing year by year is different. The £100,000 cash outflow in Year 0 is represented by the £25,000 depreciation charges in each of the Years 1–4.

This concept of the cash flow being the profit before charging depreciation, but after charging tax, is somewhat similar to the cash flows used in DCF appraisals. The latter cash flows exclude dividend and interest payments to the providers of capital as such rewards are taken into account when setting the target rate of return to use in the discounting process.

Apart from depreciation there are other reasons why the appraisal cash flows do not equate with the profit in the same year and these reasons relate to the precise timing of the transactions. A project can commence at any time in a company accounting year and therefore Year 1 of a DCF appraisal will be unlikely to cover the same twelve months used for the firm's annual accounts. Also the profit and loss account shows the tax payable on the profit of the same period. In practice most tax is paid in the following accounting year and this later payment of tax must be fully recognized as discussed in the next chapter.

The final reason is that a DCF appraisal includes cash

flows representing the outlay and subsequent recovery of working capital. Working capital is the amount of finance needed to prime the production process by paying for the materials and labour costs before cash is eventually received from the customer. The longer the production cycle and the longer customers take to pay the more working capital will be needed as cash is not recycled so quickly. In many industries the working capital cycle takes a few months from first paying out cash on wages and materials to the actual receipt of cash from credit customers. If by magic this length of time could be halved then only half of the original working capital would be needed.

Such working capital requirements never appear in a profit and loss account but are important cash flows in DCF appraisals of new products. By including working capital in the cash flows we take account of the fact that profit does not equate with the net cash inflow from sales because of the credit allowed by suppliers and the credit granted to customers. Fluctuations in such working capital items explain why the cash flow calculated from the profit plus depreciation was described as approximate on a previous page.

The best overall guideline to follow when compiling DCF cash flows is to put each item of the cash flows in the year the actual cash transaction takes place. In this way depreciation will be excluded, delays in making tax payments taken into account and working capital requirements shown.

The following list shows the most common types of cash flows to be included in an appraisal and may be useful when trying to determine which cash flows are relevant on any one project:

Figure 3.2 Checklist of types of cash flow

- Investment in replacement or additional physical assets, e.g. buildings, plant and machinery, vehicles.
- Opportunity cost of existing physical assets to be used (see later).
- Working capital requirements, i.e. stocks and debtors less creditors.

- Sales revenue.
- Operating costs, e.g. labour, materials, energy, maintenance.
- Grants receivable, e.g. regional development grant.
- Tax payments on profits.
- Tax savings on allowances.
- Scrap or resale value less disposal costs.

Which cash flows are relevant?

Relevant cash flows are all the additional costs and income which will result if the proposed investment goes ahead. These are sometimes called the incremental cash flows as they exclude existing costs on the grounds that they do not result from the investment now being appraised. This is the reason we do not apportion existing fixed overheads like rent and rates to projects because such costs continue irrespective of this project's acceptance or rejection. They result from previous decisions and should not be charged against a new project.

An exception to this rule may appear to occur when an existing asset will be sold if the proposed investment does not proceed. For example, a firm rents premises for £150,000 p.a. but could now sublet an unused part of the buildings for £50,000 or, alternatively, use the space to produce a new product. In this case the £50,000 p.a. is a valid cash flow to include in the new product appraisal. This type of cost is known as the 'opportunity cost' for the obvious reason that it is the cost of the opportunity forgone.

Another example of this opportunity cost frequently occurs when a new project can utilize existing machinery which would otherwise be sold. Here again the sale price of the machinery is taken as a relevant cash flow on this project because a similar amount of cash would have to be spent on another machine if this one had not been available.

It is important to realize that it is the present worth of an existing asset which should be counted as the cash flow. The original cost or written down value of the asset is irrelevant in a DCF appraisal. Any costs that were incurred in the past are 'sunk costs' and should not affect decisions that are made now. Only the current disposal value, or opportunity cost if put to alternative use, is relevant at this point of time.

Timing of the cash flows

Normal practice is to set out the relevant cash flows for a project on a yearly basis. The initial investment takes place at Year 0 which is in effect the start of Year 1. This may be the sole cash outflow or, as in the case of a large project involving construction and commissioning phases, there may be negative cash flows for the first two or three years. Subsequently the cash flows will turn positive as the benefits of the investment accrue. However, a negative net cash flow can arise in any one year that replacement or additional investment takes place. Typical patterns of cash flows may be:

Figure 3.3 Typical cash flow pattern of a simple project

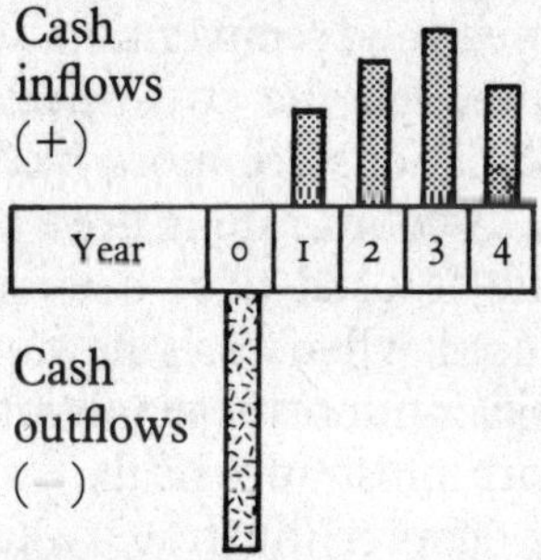

Typical cash flow pattern of a complex project

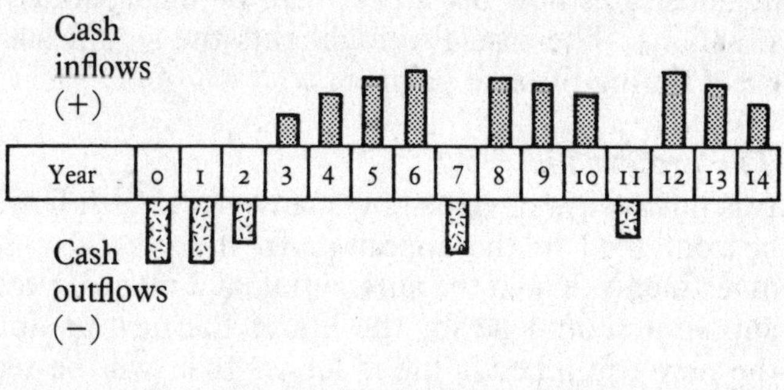

The 'present value' factors discussed in the previous chapter are used to bring future years' cash flows back to the same time value as at Year 0. By multiplying the future cash flow by a PV factor we are deducting interest for the waiting time. These PV factors are based on a whole year's interest charge on the assumption that the cash transaction takes place on the last day of the year as opposed to a continuous flow throughout the year. In the case of discrete receipts and payments of cash, for example on the purchase of an asset or the receipt of a grant, this approach would be valid. In the case of receipts from everyday sales or payments for labour, materials and other expenses this approach is less valid because of the continuous nature of such cash transactions throughout the year.

A PV factor table exists which is calculated on the assumption that cash flows take place throughout the year rather than on the last day. Ideally we should use both tables in tandem, applying each to the relevant type of cash flow within one project. In practice firms normally use only one table based on the year-end convention for all cash flows, as the difference between the two tables is not regarded as significant. Calculations are more likely to differ significantly where a high discount rate is used over a short life or a low discount rate is used over a long life. This alternative table can be used when cash flows are known with more certainty and exact interest calculations are more crucial than is the case with most appraisals.

A later example in this chapter illustrates a lease or buy appraisal whilst Case Study No. 1 at the end of the book demonstrates how tax aspects can be incorporated in such situations. The case also highlights the significance of the exact timing of lease payments.

The project life

It is not always obvious how many years' cash flows should be contained in the appraisal. In the case of cost saving investments, say in the automation of a manual process, the appraisal should be for the life of the new equipment. If the new equipment's life is longer than will be required a residual value can be assumed at the end of the project's life. This will show as a cash inflow in the last year.

When appraising new products the project life can be taken as either the product life or the plant life, whichever is the shorter. If the plant life exceeds the product life a residual value, if any, can be assumed as above. If the product life exceeds the plant life the plant replacement can be built into the cash flow in the year required. In complex production systems all the plant items will not wear out simultaneously so a number of replacements may occur in different years. It is important to recognize that for the moment we are still assuming these replacements are at the same prices as the original plant.

Compiling the cash flows

On relatively small projects only one manager may be involved in assessing the future benefits of a proposed investment. Take the proposal to install a conveyor system to replace manual handling. An industrial engineer can probably assess the expected yearly savings over the equipment's life. In contrast, a project to build and equip a factory to sell new products is not within the compass of any one individual. A project team of an engineer, a production manager, a sales manager and an accountant will be needed to assess the yearly cash flows. Data on past performance may be useful but the application of scientific management will be more beneficial in assessing future costs and benefits. The techniques of market research, method study, work measurement and value engineering are only some of those relevant in this type of situation.

At this stage it is useful to assume that only one estimate is made of the future net cash flows. Chapter 5 discusses the problem that the future is uncertain. One suggested approach is to produce a number of sets of cash flows based on different assumptions. We also temporarily assume the absence of inflation. This unrealistic assumption is removed in Chapter 6 which explains the impact of inflation on all cash flow items and how to deal with it. Now we can examine different types of investments to see how the net cash flows are built up. Tax aspects are ignored until the following chapter.

Example of a new product appraisal

The management of Expansion Limited are considering investing £100,000 in new plant and £20,000 in working capital to make and sell a new product. Profits before charging depreciation are expected to be £45,000 in each of the four years the product will be sold. At the end of this time it is estimated the plant can be sold for £10,000 and the working capital released in full. Expansion Ltd require a return of at least 20% before approving projects of this kind.

Figure 3.4 Calculation of the net present value at 20%

Year	*Investment* £	*Profit* £	*Net cash flow* £	*PV factors @ 20%*	*PV* £
0	− 120,000		− 120,000	1.000	− 120,000
1		+ 45,000	+ 45,000	.833	+ 37,485
2		+ 45,000	+ 45,000	.694	+ 31,230
3		+ 45,000	+ 45,000	.579	+ 26,055
4	+ 30,000	+ 45,000	+ 75,000	.482	+ 36,150
				NPV	+ £10,920

The initial investment at Year 0 is £120,000, being the money spent on the plant and the working capital. This working capital needs to earn a return just as much as the investment in fixed assets. It is not released until the end of Year 4 and together with the sale proceeds of the plant totals £30,000. Cash inflows from sales less costs amount to £45,000 each year. Depreciation is not charged as the whole of the cost is included at Year 0 when the actual payment for the plant takes place. The net present value surplus of £10,920 indicates the company can expect a greater return than the 20% required. By a further trial at a higher rate and interpolation of the two NPVs the DCF yield will be found at 24%. Expansion Limited will consider this project viable as the expected return exceeds their minimum target figure.

Example of a cost saving investment

Efficient Builders Limited are contemplating how to reduce site labouring costs and are considering mechanization to drastically reduce the need for hod carriers. Their studies have indicated that a machine costing £20,000 will save labour costs of £15,000 each year. Operating and maintenance costs of the machine will amount to £6,000 in each of the five years the machine is expected to last. At the end of this time it is not expected to have any significant value. The directors do not normally approve expenditure unless at least a 25% return on investment is anticipated.

Figure 3.5 Calculation of the net present value at 25%

Year	*Investment* £	*Operating cost* £	*Savings* £	*Net cash flow* £	*PV factors @ 25%*	*PV* £
0	− 20,000			− 20,000	1.000	− 20,000
1		− 6,000	+ 15,000	+ 9,000	.800	+ 7,200
2		− 6,000	+ 15,000	+ 9,000	.640	+ 5,760
3		− 6,000	+ 15,000	+ 9,000	.512	+ 4,608
4		− 6,000	+ 15,000	+ 9,000	.410	+ 3,690
5		− 6,000	+ 15,000	+ 9,000	.328	+ 2,952
					NPV	+ £4,210

The £9,000 cash inflow in each of five years yields a return of more than the 25% required on the investment of £20,000. The DCF yield can be found by using the cumulative PV factor table when the cumulative factor is found by dividing the £20,000 investment by the £9,000 constant annual cash flow. This equals 2.222. When we look for 2.222 on the 5 year line of the cumulative table we find it equates to a DCF yield of 35%.

Sometimes it is easier to turn the question round by calculating the annual savings required to yield the 25% return required, rather than estimate one precise savings figure. In this example if we divide the £20,000 investment by the cumulative PV factor for 5 years at 25% (2.689) we find the annual cash flow needs to be £7,438. As the operating costs are £6,000 each year this means that savings in labourers' wages must exceed £13,438 before the investment will be viable. Managers may find it easier to answer the question posed in this way rather than put their head on the block by making one estimate of the expected savings.

Example of a replacement investment

You may think that a replacement decision is another cost saving investment and in many ways it is similar to the previous example. In that case the choice was whether to invest or not. Assuming the underlying activity is still required, a replacement decision is a choice both whether and when to invest. Replacement is normally indicated when the first year saving gives an adequate return if repeated over the whole life of the new asset. The following example illustrates this approach.

Modern Limited are considering replacing an existing machine with a new one to reduce operating and maintenance costs. The new machine will cost £40,000 and is expected to last ten years with only negligible value by that time. The existing machine can be sold now for £5,000. Operating and maintenance costs are currently £25,000 for the existing machine but will fall to only £18,000 each year for the new machine. Modern Limited require a return of at least 15% before sanctioning such investments.

Figure 3.6 Calculation of the net present value at 15% using the cumulative PV table

Year	*Existing costs* £	*New costs* £	*Net cash flow* £	*PV factors at 15%*	*PV* £
0	− 5,000	− 40,000	− 35,000	1.000	− 35,000
1–10	− 25,000	− 18,000	+ 7,000	5.019	+ 35,133
				NPV	+ £133

The additional or incremental investment is £35,000, being the cost of the new machine less the sale proceeds from the old. Resulting from the modernization is a saving in running costs of £7,000 in each of the next ten years. This gives a NPV surplus of £133 at 15% which is so near zero we can assume the DCF yield to be almost exactly 15%. The proposed investment is therefore very marginal as it is expected to yield only the minimum required return. If Modern Ltd had been seeking a higher rate of return than 15% the replacement would not be viable as the yearly savings of £7,000 would not give an adequate return on the £35,000 investment. Conversely, if the company is satisfied with a lower return than 15% the replacement would be viable.

Replacement situations are not always so easy to evaluate. We may be faced with increasing running costs as the machines grow older. These future costs must therefore be estimated. It may be necessary to repair or overhaul the existing machine to extend its useful life. These repair and overhaul costs need to be assessed. Any such extended life of the existing machine is unlikely to be as long as the life of a new machine. Ways have to be found to compare like with like over a common period. This can be effected either by comparing the yearly costs of old and new machines or by comparing their PV cost over the lowest common denominator number of years. A further complication can arise if an improved specification will be available if replacement is deferred another year or two. When appraising replacement situations the alternative courses of action must be identified and assessed. Care must be taken to ensure the comparisons are valid and the above points considered where relevant. Case Study No. 2 examines a replacement situation where running costs increase each year and the life of the replacement machine exceeds that of the existing machine.

Example of choice between alternatives

In the previous chapter we saw that projects can be ranked in order of attractiveness, either by the profitability index when using the NPV method or by the size of the DCF yield. Care must be taken when selecting the best investment from a range of alternatives because the largest profitability index or DCF yield is not necessarily the one selected in this special situation. Alternative investments occur when the acceptance of one project precludes the acceptance of an alternative scheme to achieve similar ends. Such projects are sometimes referred to as 'mutually exclusive' schemes.

The basic rule to follow is to choose the alternative with the highest NPV surplus at the required rate of return. An equally valid approach is to calculate the return on the extra, or incremental, cost of the dearer alternative, to decide whether it is worth investing the extra money. The following example demonstrates these methods.

Carriers Limited are trying to decide between two transporters which are both satisfactory from a technical viewpoint but which have different costs and benefits. Model A costs £40,000 and its payload is expected to earn £10,200 in each of the next ten years. Model B costs £30,000 but its earning capacity is only £8,400 each year for the same life. Carriers management want to know which is the better buy.

Figure 3.7 *Calculations of DCF yields and net present values at various rates of interest*

	Year 0 £	*Years 1–10* £	*DCF yield*	*NPV @ 30%* £	*NPV @ 20%* £	*NPV @ 8%* £
Model A	− 40,000	+ 10,200	22%	− 8,462	+ 2,758	+ 28,442
Model B	− 30,000	+ 8,400	25%	− 4,027	+ 5,213	+ 26,364
Increment	− 10,000	+ 1,800	12%	− 4,435	− 2,455	+ 2,078

The above analysis shows that Model A gives a DCF yield of 22% whilst Model B gives a return of 25%. If Carriers Ltd require a return on new investments higher than either of these figures then neither investment is worthwhile. This is also illustrated by both NPVs being negative at an assumed target rate of 30%. However, at a lower required rate of return, say 20%, both projects appear satisfactory as their DCF yields exceed this target figure. The higher NPV surplus at this rate is achieved by Model B which also has the higher DCF yield and will be the one selected.

If Carriers Limited were looking for a relatively low rate

of return, say 8%, Model A now has the higher NPV surplus notwithstanding its DCF yield of 22% being lower than the 25% of Model B. This accords with the basic rule stipulated above that the project with the highest NPV surplus at the required rate of return should be selected from a group of mutually exclusive schemes. Therefore Model A should be selected even though its rate of profitability is the lower overall when measured by the DCF yield.

This apparent paradox can be explained by looking at the difference in costs and revenues of the two models. The incremental or extra cost of the investment in Model A is £10,000. The return on this investment is £1,800 yearly for the ten year life, which equates to a DCF yield of 12%. We can think of Model A as being the combination of Model B and the increment. Model B is acceptable with a DCF yield of 25% and the return of 12% on the incremental investment is more than the 8% postulated. Therefore Model A is preferred because it achieves everything Model B offers in addition to an acceptable return on the extra investment of £10,000. If the target rate were set higher than the 12% achieved by the incremental investment this would no longer be the case and Model B would now be preferred. This would leave the firm with £10,000 to invest in another project which satisfied the higher criterion rate.

Example of a financing decision

Modern Limited has decided to acquire the replacement machine outlined in a previous example at a net cost of £35,000. The manufacturer has offered leasing terms as an alternative to outright purchase. The leasing agreement stipulates yearly payments of £6,500 for each of the ten years. In total these payments amount to £65,000 and appear much dearer than outright purchase. When the timing of the payments over the years is taken into account their present value cost is only £32,623 (£6,500 × 5.019) allowing for a 15% interest rate. This £32,623 is the sum of money needed to withdraw £6,500 at the end of each year to make the leasing payment, whilst leaving the balance to accumulate interest at 15% compounded yearly. In this instance leasing is the more attractive alternative as £32,623 is considerably cheaper than outright purchase at £35,000.

The point has previously been made that the timing of leasing payments within any one year can be critical. If the leasing payments occurred at the beginning of each year their total present value cost would amount to £37,518 which is significantly more. This is calculated by multiplying the £6,500 by the cumulative factor 5.772 (1.000 + 4.772). It is more likely in practice that the leasing payments will be made periodically during each year. In this case their present value cost amounts to £33,676 which is found by use of a further table. This is not so significantly different from the £32,623 figure obtained by use of the year-end factors.

Non-taxpaying organizations will appraise the choice between lease or buy in the above manner. They may find leasing terms attractive if these reflect the tax allowance obtainable by the finance company which is denied themselves. Case Study No. 1 includes tax aspects in a lease or buy appraisal as they apply to taxpaying private sector firms. It also discusses the timing of the leasing payments.

Conclusions

Simple financial models can be constructed for any investment situation showing the expected cash inflow or outflow on a yearly basis. The worthwhileness of the investment is found by allowing for the time value of money through the discounting process. Any investment that is more than repaid in present value terms is worthwhile.

All the examples illustrated in this chapter have omitted to take into account taxation, uncertainty and inflation. The following three chapters deal with each of these aspects in turn. In them we adjust the yearly cash flows for their effects to make the appraisals completely realistic.

4 Is tax a cash flow?

Some of the most important decisions managers make are those concerning whether and when to invest, particularly if large amounts of capital are involved. Tax rates and tax allowances are both at high levels in the UK and form an important part of the economic environment in which firms operate. The value and timing of tax transactions will significantly affect the rate of return on any investment.

As managers you should be aware of the significance of these tax matters and how they will affect your firm. To be otherwise means you may not always spot profitable opportunities if they arise nor fully judge their merits when they do.

The existence of a central government with the power to levy taxes means that it can influence firms' investment decisions through the tax system. Cash flows on any project will be incomplete if we do not build the tax effects into the yearly figures. There are two aspects to taxation, one being negative and the other positive. The negative side is the payment of tax on profits whilst the positive side is the receipt of tax allowances which reduce the tax payments.

Corporation tax is the system of taxation which applies to profits of all limited companies and nationalized industries, as opposed to income tax which applies to profits of the self-employed and partnerships. Differences between the two systems are confined mainly to the tax rates and the timing of the tax payments. If we examine the principles of corporation tax first then the differences of the income tax system can be contrasted later.

There are two rates of corporation tax, either of which can apply, depending on the size of the taxable profit for the year. The normal rate is 52% at the time of writing but a small companies rate of 40% exists for firms whose profits are relatively low. There is a gradual increase in the rate from 40% to 52% which applies to companies whose profits fall within the band where the 40% rate ceases to apply but the full 52% rate is not yet applicable. Usually the Chancellor increases these limits in his spring budget but the actual rates of corporation tax are rarely altered. Even when they are altered it is normally too late for a company to take action as the rate of tax announced in the budget is retrospective for the tax year ending about the same time.

The accounting year for many companies will not cover the same twelve months as the tax year which runs from 1 April one year to the following 31 March. If the rate of tax did alter from one tax year to the next and the company accounting year straddled both tax years, then the year's profit is apportioned *pro rata* for the number of months which fall into each tax year. The two rates of tax can then be levied on the respective part of the profit which falls into each tax year as follows:

Figure 4.1 Apportionment of year's profit over two tax years

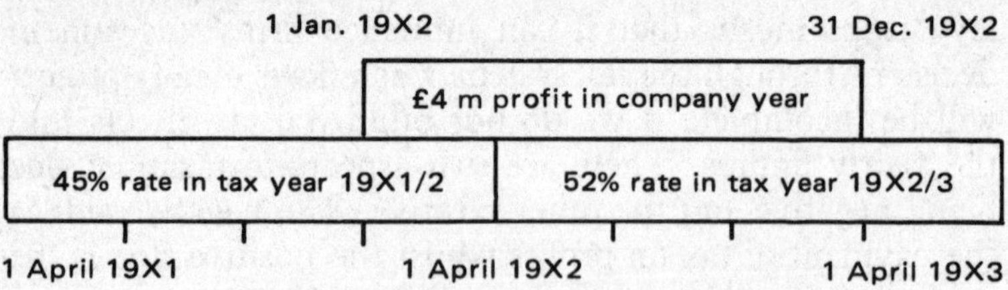

Tax payable on £4 m profit = ($^1/_4$ × £4 m) 45% + ($^3/_4$ × £4 m) 52%

The profit on which corporation tax is levied (£4 m in the above example) is not identical with the profit disclosed in the firm's profit and loss account but is an adjusted profit figure after some costs have been disallowed and some other allowances received. The statement in Figure 4.2 shows the main adjustments that take place.

It can be seen from this statement that there are significant adjustments which affect the taxable profit. Depreciation charged by your company in its profit and loss account is added back to profit as though it had never been de-

Figure 4.2 Corporation tax assessment

		£
Profit as per profit & loss account		900,000
Add back disallowed expenses:	£	
Depreciation	200,000	
Entertainment	10,000	
Political contributions	5,000	
Provision for possible bad debts	1,000	216,000
		1,116,000
Deduct:		
Capital allowances	306,000	
Stock relief	110,000	416,000
Taxable profit		£700,000

Corporation tax payable is
£700,000 × 52% = £364,000

ducted. It is *never* possible therefore to reduce the size of the tax bill by charging extra depreciation in any one year large profits happen to be made. Whatever figure a company charges for depreciation the Inland Revenue will add back. The taxable profit each year is sales less all allowable operating costs excluding depreciation. Referring back to Figure 3.1 in the previous chapter the taxable profit in that case was £50,000 p.a. being the sales of £200,000 p.a. less operating costs of £150,000 p.a. The depreciation of £25,000 p.a. on the plant is not deducted as it is neither a cash outflow nor an allowable expense for tax purposes.

It would be unfair if companies were disallowed depreciation and given nothing in its place. Depreciation is the yearly charge for buildings, plant and machinery, vehicles and office equipment. The only difference between these costs, as opposed to paying for wages and materials, is the time they last. Firms could not provide goods and services to customers without investing in these physical assets, unless they chose to lease them. In this case the lease or rent payments are included as expenses in the profit and loss account and tax relief is automatically obtained.

Capital allowances

The Inland Revenue have their own system of depreciation allowances which are called capital allowances or writing down allowances. These are available to firms which buy new physical assets of the specified categories, although some allowances are restricted to specific industries only. The following is a list of the current rates of capital allowances:

Figure 4.3 Rates of capital allowances as at March 1981

Industrial buildings	75% initial allowance plus 4% p.a. annual allowance up to 100% max.
Hotel buildings (10 bedrooms +)	20% initial allowance plus 4% p.a. annual allowance up to 100% max.
Plant and machinery, equipment and vehicles (excluding cars)	100% initial allowance
Motor cars	25% p.a. annual allowance based on reducing capital value (subject to a limit)

The capital allowances on industrial and hotel buildings are restricted to firms operating in the specified Standard Industrial Classifications. The remaining allowances apply to all industries. From the above it can be deduced that no allowance is given for buildings used by service industries (with the exception of new hotel buildings) although the equipment, furniture and vehicles they use are eligible. A deviation to this rule occurred in 1981 with the introduction of 'enterprise zones'. New commercial buildings in these areas qualify for an initial allowance of 100%.

It may have struck you that the size of some of these tax allowances is significantly higher than the equivalent depreciation rate used for charging depreciation in the firm's profit and loss account. Take for example a new factory costing £4 m and expected to last forty years. Depreciation will amount to 1/40th or $2^1/_2$% p.a. of the £4 m which equals £100,000 p.a. The tax allowance in the first year will be (75% + 4%) of £4 m = £3.16 m and 4% of £4 m =

£160,000 p.a. for each of the next 5¼ years. Obviously the Chancellor is not just substituting his capital allowance for the company's depreciation but is using the allowances as investment incentives to influence economic activity generally.

In the case of plant and machinery this acceleration is even more marked because 100% of the cost is deductible from profits in the year of acquisition. Using as an illustration an item of plant costing £100,000, at the end of the accounting year you can reduce your taxable profits by this £100,000 and thereby save a tax payment of £52,000, being the capital allowance of £100,000 × 52% corporation tax rate. In subsequent years, however, no tax allowance will be available because it has all been claimed in the first year. To keep tax bills down in later years your company will have to keep on investing in new assets. The following illustration shows how in Year 2 the effective tax rate can rise above 52% when the depreciation that is disallowed is not offset by an equal amount of capital allowances. The more likely situation is the opposite when the capital allowances exceed the depreciation and the effective rate of tax falls below 52% as in Year 1:

Figure 4.4 Variations in the effective rate of tax

	Year 1 £	*Year 2* £
Profit as per profit & loss account	400,000	400,000
Add back: depreciation	60,000	80,000
	460,000	480,000
Deduct: 100% capital allowance on equipment	100,000	Nil
Taxable profit	360,000	480,000
Corporation tax at 52%	187,200	249,600
Effective rate of tax on original profit	46.8%	62.4%

In Year 2 when no new investment in equipment takes place, a higher depreciation charge is added back because of the previous year's new purchase. No allowances are available in this later year if no new investment takes place as 100% allowances have already been claimed in previous years on existing equipment. The bigger the gap between allowances and depreciation relative to the size of the original profit then the more the effective rate of tax will vary from the basic rate of tax.

Tax allowances on motor cars are more likely to coincide with the firm's practice on depreciation. Most firms use the 25% writing down allowance on reducing capital balance when calculating their own depreciation charge to include in the profit and loss account. Managers are no longer able to run a Rolls-Royce at the expense of other taxpayers because tax allowances are restricted to a maximum figure which effectively excludes all luxury vehicles. In the case of a car costing £8,000 the following allowances apply:

Figure 4.5
25% capital allowances on reducing value of £8,000 car

	£	
Purchase cost of car	8,000	
Year 1 – capital allowance	2,000	(25% of £8,000)
Written down value – Year 1	6,000	
Year 2 – capital allowance	1,500	(25% of £6,000)
Written down value – Year 2	4,500	
Year 3 – capital allowance	1,125	(25% of £4,500)
Written down value – Year 3	3,375	

The annual allowance falls substantially each year but the written down value never reaches zero. Whenever the asset is sold a balancing up with the Inland Revenue takes place. If we assume the above car was sold after three years use it is unlikely it would exactly realize its book value of £3,375. If it was sold for £3,000 the Inland Revenue would give a 'balancing allowance' of the £375 difference. On the other hand if the car realized £3,800 the taxman would claim back the excess allowances of £425 previously granted. This 'balancing charge' would result in the firm paying back £425 × 52% = £221 tax when it settled the tax bill for the year in which the sale took place. In the case of plant where a 100% capital allowance has already been received the Inland Revenue tax the scrap or sale proceeds as a 'balancing charge'.

When appraising projects the availability of these tax allowances must be incorporated in the cash flows. Tax saved by claiming these allowances will occur in the year the payment would otherwise have taken place. We must now look to see when tax is due for payment.

Tax payments

One of the good things we can say about tax on limited company profits is that it is not payable immediately, but after a time lag. The present system of corporation tax goes back to 1972 and is called an 'imputation system'. When a limited company makes a dividend payment it pays a 'net' dividend to shareholders and a tax payment to the Inland Revenue. For example, on a net dividend of £700 the tax payment is £300 ($^3/_7$ths) being equivalent to income tax at the 30% standard rate. Such tax is deemed to be an advance payment of the company's total corporation tax liability. The shareholder receives the net dividend of £700 together with a 'tax credit' of £300, so his total or gross dividend is £1,000. If the shareholder is not liable for tax he can claim this £300 back from the Inland Revenue. Conversely, if he is liable for higher rates of tax than the 30% already paid on his behalf, he will receive a further tax bill in due course.

Most companies make two dividend payments within any twelve months, namely the interim and final dividend relating to their accounting year. This results in two payments of 'advance corporation tax' or ACT being made. The interim dividend payment takes place after the first half-year profits are known, which may be about nine months after the start of the accounting year. The final dividend payment normally takes place after the annual general meeting has approved the directors' recommendation, which will be at least three months after the accounting year end. At this stage the total tax liability for the accounting year is computed along the lines of Figure 4.2 and agreed with the

Inspector of Taxes. The previous payments of ACT are deducted from this total tax liability to arrive at the balance or 'mainstream' tax payable. This last payment will not be due until at least nine months after the company year end, or even longer in the case of a company incorporated before 5 April 1965 when corporation tax started. It is possible for the delay to be anything up to twenty-one months after the company year end.

The nature of the above three tax payments relating to profits of any one year makes it very difficult to generalize about exactly when tax is paid. It depends on the proportion of profit paid out as dividends as well as when the company was formed. When appraising investments we need to incorporate tax payments in the yearly cash flows. A good rule of thumb is to assume an average delay of one year in the payment of all tax on profits. Taking the example first illustrated in Figure 3.4 the taxable profits in that case were the £45,000 yearly cash inflows. Assuming total company profits make the company liable for tax at the normal rate of 52%, the following cash flows emerge when the tax payments are lagged one year:

Figure 4.6 Cash flows incorporating 52% tax payments on profits

Year	*Taxable profit* £	*Tax @ 52%* £	*Net cash flow* £
1	+ 45,000	—	+ 45,000
2	+ 45,000	− 23,400	+ 21,600
3	+ 45,000	− 23,400	+ 21,600
4	+ 45,000	− 23,400	+ 21,600
5		− 23,400	− 23,400

Because tax payments are made in arrears, the benefit of deducting capital allowances from profits to reduce these tax payments must also be delayed. Any capital allowances a firm can deduct from its year's profit will reduce the mainstream tax payment rather than ACT payments which are solely dictated by the size of the dividend.

In an individual project appraisal where we need to include as a cash inflow the tax saved by claiming capital allowances, it is necessary to allow either a one or two year time lag. This is because the investment takes place at Year 0, being the beginning of the project's first year. If this happened to be near the end of the company accounting year the delay could be only nine months but could, alternatively, be up to twenty-one months for a long established company. If the investment took place at the start of the company accounting year the tax saving could be between 21 and 33 months away. Within your own company you may be able to make a more precise estimate of these delays in tax transactions.

Another point to consider is whether firms are taxed project by project or as a total entity. We need to incorporate tax savings and payments in each project appraisal but in reality firms are taxed on the total profit less allowances for the whole firm. In some cases a number of firms in one group may be taxed as one entity. If the firm's total profit is large enough to offset all available capital allowances then we do not have to offset the allowances of one project against only that project's profits. We can effect a saving in the tax paid by the whole entity and show this as a cash inflow on the project.

Referring again to Figure 3.4 let us assume a 100% capital allowance is available on the £100,000 investment in new plant. This will have the effect of reducing the company tax bill by £52,000 in Year 2 provided the whole company profit in Year 1 exceeded the £100,000 allowance. (A two year lag has been assumed in the absence of more specific information.) When the plant is resold at the end of Year 4 the Inland Revenue claim back tax on the £10,000 sale proceeds as a balancing charge. Excluding working capital, the net cash flows will now be as in Figure 4.7.

In this example the benefit gained by saving tax on the allowance is only possible where profits already exist in the rest of the company equal to the size of the allowance claimed. The other possibility is that there are no existing company profits against which to offset the capital allowance of this one project. In this case the allowance will have to be claimed over the number of years it takes the project's

Figure 4.7 Cash flows incorporating 100% capital allowance on plant assuming immediate claim possible

Year	Investment	Taxable profits	52% tax on profit	Capital allowance	Tax saved on allowance	Total tax payable	Net cash flow
	£	£	£		£	£	£
0	− 100,000			100,000			− 100,000
1		+ 45,000					+ 45,000
2		+ 45,000	− 23,400		+ 52,000	+ 28,600	+ 73,600
3		+ 45,000	− 23,400			− 23,400	+ 21,600
4	+ 10,000	+ 45,000	− 23,400	(10,000)		− 23,400	+ 31,600
5			− 23,400		− 5,200	− 28,600	− 28,600

profits to equal the size of the allowance. Using the same example the cash flows will now appear as:

Figure 4.8 Cash flows incorporating 100% capital allowance on plant assuming immediate claim not possible

Year	Investment	Taxable profits	52% tax on profit	Capital allowance	Tax saved on allowance	Total tax payable	Net cash flow
	£	£	£		£	£	£
0	− 100,000						− 100,000
1		+ 45,000		45,000			+ 45,000
2		+ 45,000	− 23,400	45,000	+ 23,400	nil	+ 45,000
3		+ 45,000	− 23,400	10,000	+ 23,400	nil	+ 45,000
4	+ 10,000	+ 45,000	− 23,400	(10,000)	+ 5,200	− 18,200	+ 36,800
5			− 23,400		− 5,200	− 28,600	− 28,600

In both the above illustrations the total tax payable amounts to the same figure over the project's life but the ability to claim the tax allowance more quickly, as in Figure 4.7, will result in a higher rate of return after discounting. The tax rate applicable to the size of profits in Figure 4.8 should really be the small company rate of 40%, but it has been left at 52% for the purpose of comparison with Figure 4.7.

A comprehensive example of an expansion project incorporating aspects of taxation in an inflationary environment is contained in Case Study No. 3 at the end of this book.

Regional development grant (RDG)

Strictly speaking these have nothing to do with taxation as their administration comes under the auspices of the Department of Industry rather than the Inland Revenue. They are included in this section because of the involvement with government but also because some confusion can occur as to their tax treatment. An RDG is an out-and-out subsidy. It is a cash grant to manufacturing firms to persuade them to invest in new plant and machinery and to build new factories in areas of high unemployment.

Qualifying firms in Special Development Areas, for example, can claim an RDG of 22% at the time of writing based on the cost of new plant and industrial buildings. The whole cost of such investments is borne by the firm in full initially, as a time lag of about one year occurs after the audited claim has been submitted until receipt of the grant. It is important to realize that such grants are tax free and do not affect the capital allowances which are still calculated on the full cost. Other incentives apply to the remaining economic areas and various grants and allowances are available from local authorities particularly for small firms and investments creating new employment. Managers should check out all available sources of assistance before embarking on a new project as prior approval is needed in most instances. Once the value and timing of the assistance has been determined it is incorporated in the yearly cash flows.

Stock relief

Since the early 1970s various systems of tax relief have been applied to increases in a firm's stocks and work-in-progress to help the firm finance their inflated cost. Originally the relief applied to the increase in both volume and price thus giving firms an incentive to stockpile at year ends. When stocks fell at a year end, however, it left them with a potential liability to repay stock relief previously granted when the taxman applied clawback.

A new system of stock relief has been introduced from November 1980 until such time, if ever, the Inland Revenue taxes profits which have been totally adjusted for inflation, as outlined in Chapter 6. The stock relief now available reduces taxable profits by the increased money value of the stock which existed at the start of the accounting year. This is calculated by reference to a special price index compiled by the Central Statistical Office and published in *Price Index Numbers for Current Cost Accounting*. The effect is to measure the impact of inflation, over the year, on the stock which existed at the start of the year and reduce the taxable profits accordingly. In this way companies will not be taxed on profits they must retain to finance the inflated money value of stocks.

A small amount of stock (currently £2,000) is ignored in this computation to avoid the taxman getting bogged down with too many small claims. Where stocks are large (currently over £1 m) the relief is reduced by the proportion of borrowings to total assets. This takes the view that the owners of a company do not bear the whole inflation burden on stocks if those stocks are partly financed by borrowing and not all by shareholders' funds. For example, assume that a firm has an opening stock of £4 m and total assets at the year end of £10 m. These assets are financed £7 m by owners capital and £3 m by borrowings. The increase in the special price index for stocks was 10% for the year:

Stock relief = (opening stock – £2,000) × change in special price index for stocks × borrowing restriction
= (£4,000,000–£2,000) × 10% × $(1-{}^{3}/_{10})$
= £279,860 which amount is deducted from profits before calculating the tax payable.

There is no tax allowance on the basic investment in stocks or other working capital items. Only when inflation exists will tax relief be granted on the inflated value of the stock. If a firm stockpiles at the year end it will have to wait a further year to claim the effects of inflation on that stock and obtain stock relief via a lower tax payment at least a further year hence. Because of the long time lag, this present system of stock relief does not induce firms to stockpile at year ends as much as the previous system which gave quicker relief for the increased volume of stock as well as its inflated value.

Working capital is included in a project appraisal as a

cash outflow in the years it is required, usually starting at Year 0. It is shown as a cash inflow in the years it is reduced or totally recovered at the end of the project's life. These transactions are necessary because the firm has to earn a return on the working capital just as much as on the fixed investment in plant or buildings. There are no tax allowances or tax payments to build into the cash flows regarding stocks or working capital in total. The only exception is where inflation exists and stock relief is available as a consequence. In this case the cash flows on the project should include both the additional working capital requirements brought about by inflation each year and the reduced tax payments incorporating stock relief. Working capital is further examined in Chapter 6, which discusses all aspects of inflation, whilst a worked example is contained in Case Study No. 3.

Public authorities
Corporation tax applies to nationalized industries and they should allow for payment of tax and the benefit of capital allowances in their project appraisals. In some cases nationalized industries have large accumulated capital allowances they have not been able to offset against profits in previous years. It would be unrealistic to allow for tax payments and allowances in the normal way. A suggested approach is to offset the allowances against the taxable profits in the way outlined in Figure 4.8. If the level of future profits and the size of unused past allowances are such that it is envisaged the nationalized industry will never be liable for tax payments, then it is advisable to exclude tax completely from the cash flows. This will also be the case with local authorities, water authorities and similar bodies which are specifically excluded from corporation tax.

Taxing the self-employed
Previous discussion has centred on limited companies which come under the auspices of the corporation tax system. Some businessmen, however, trade in their own name, or as a partnership, without ever forming a limited company.

Profits of these self-employed persons come under the income tax system which also applies to employees. Unlike limited companies, the self-employed do not pay dividends and any drawings or salary they pay themselves are not allowed when computing the taxable profit.

Profits from running a business are deemed to be the income of the individual or partner. Like limited companies, the various capital allowances on new investment and the stock relief system previously mentioned all apply. The remaining profits are taxed in bands at rates presently varying from 30% to 60% after the personal allowances for the particular individual have been deducted.

Collection of income tax from employees takes place weekly or monthly under the PAYE system. The Inland Revenue cannot operate the same system with the self-employed because the income or profits are not known until the accounting year ends. In practice it takes a few months to prepare and audit accounts so the delay is even longer. To overcome this problem the Inland Revenue charges income tax in the current year based on the level of profits earned in the previous tax year. More precisely the normal basis of assessment for ongoing self-employed firms is to take the profits of the accounting year ended in the previous tax year as the basis for assessing tax payable in the current tax year. This is known as the 'preceding year' basis. Because current profits can never be available, tax is based on out-of-date figures. This does not mean that there is a long delay in the payment of tax but simply that current tax is based on an outdated figure. The actual payment of tax is made 50% on 1 January in the current tax year and the remaining 50% on 1 July which actually falls in the next tax year.

Taking the example of a self-employed person whose accounting year ends 31 August, the profit for the accounting year ended 31 August 1982 falls in the tax year 1982/83. This profit will be used as the basis for assessing income tax for the tax year 1983/84 which tax will be payable equally on 1 January 1984 and 1 July 1984.

When incorporating tax payments and tax savings into

discounted cash flow appraisals the timing must be taken into account. If profits are constant each year then the correct amount of tax will be paid within three months of the year end and no delay in payment should be assumed. Tax in this case is a cash outflow in the same year as the profit (before charging depreciation) is shown as a cash inflow. Where profits are not constant each year there will still be a cash outflow for tax each year but the current year's tax payment should be based on the previous year's profit figure. This is not the same case as limited companies where we assumed a delay of one year in the payment of tax. In the case of self-employed persons there is no delay of one year but the size of the previous year's profits determines the size of the current year's tax payment. A time lag of one year should be assumed, however, when incorporating the benefit of capital allowances into the net cash flows.

A practical difficulty occurs here when the size of the profits is such that higher rates of tax are payable. The benefit of capital allowances shows up in reduced taxable profits, starting at the highest rate of tax which would have been payable if the investment had not taken place. If the size of the capital allowances is such that a number of bands of taxable income are eliminated then the tax saved should be calculated at the different marginal rates of tax applicable in that case.

Capital gains tax (CGT)

A capital gain takes place when a possession like a building is sold for more than the firm paid for it. Such a gain is taxable at the one rate of 30%. In the case of a limited company any CGT is included in the corporation tax assessment but a self-employed person will receive a separate CGT assessment. CGT does not apply to profits made from the firm's normal trading activity but only includes profits from the sale of fixed assets and investments.

In practice firms rarely pay this tax because of 'roll-over relief' which allows them to buy new fixed assets of any kind with the total sale proceeds of the old. This defers the tax on the original capital gain until the new acquisition is eventually disposed of in its turn. As this process can be repeated without limit CGT is not normally a problem for companies. An exception might occur on the 'sale and lease-back' of freehold premises if the firm needs the sale proceeds to pay off debts or increase its working capital as opposed to buying new fixed assets. In this case CGT will be payable as 'roll-over relief' does not apply.

Value added tax (VAT)
This tax has little influence on investment decisions. Cash flows on a project should be expressed net of any VAT as the tax paid on purchased items is offset against tax charged on sales to customers. The company merely acts as a tax collector when it pays over the balance of tax to the Customs and Excise each quarter. It is possible for a firm to be out of pocket temporarily if it pays VAT on suppliers' invoices and the balance of VAT to the government before it has received VAT from its own customers. In this case additional working capital may be required and should be allowed for in the cash flows of relevant projects.

Conclusions
When appraising the worthwhileness of any investment, the effects of tax must be taken into account. Tax allowances and payments pull in opposite directions but their existence and timing can significantly affect the rate of return on a project. As managers you should be aware of these consequences of government intervention and take them fully into account in your decision-making role.

5 How certain can we be about the future?

It would be unrealistic for us to assume that the future events, expressed in one set of yearly cash flows, will occur exactly as predicted. Only in a few situations, for example when leasing premises or investing in government securities, will we be confident the expected cash flows will take place as planned. The past is known with certainty but the nature of investment appraisal is such that we will always be dealing with an uncertain future. There is therefore an element of risk about the investments most firms undertake. Risk occurs because income, costs, tax, inflation or the life of the project may not turn out as originally estimated. Some writers differentiate between risk and uncertainty along the lines that risk can be quantified but uncertainty cannot. It is intended here to use the terms synonymously.

Previous chapters have attempted to demonstrate the superiority of discounting techniques in assessing the worthwhileness of investments. This superiority stems from taking each year's cash flow into account over the whole life of the project. There is the danger that managers are tempted to use crude, simple techniques when evaluating projects, on the grounds that the data is far from certain. In short they justify poor methods by the poor data on which they are performed. Such an approach ignores the major contribution DCF techniques can make to management decision making in the field of uncertainty.

When projects are overwhelmingly profitable it does not matter which appraisal techniques are used. They are viable on any test we care to apply. Most projects, however, are more marginal and subject to a greater degree of uncertainty. It is the role of DCF techniques, not only to say how profitable a project is expected to be, but also how likely such profitability will be achieved, that is of the greatest assistance to managers. The more substantial a project is, relative to the size of the firm, the more sifting should be done before approval is given. Very often (as with marriage) it is a case of 'invest in haste – repent at leisure'!

This chapter discusses various alternative approaches firms take to the problems of risk and uncertainty. It demonstrates the advantages of DCF allied techniques and the use of computers for repetitive calculations.

Payback period

Chapter 2 described payback as a crude technique used to measure the worthwhileness of investments. This is performed by counting the number of years it takes to recover the cost of the original investment. Sometimes firms use payback in a slightly different context to reduce the risk element in a project by setting a maximum allowable payback period. The advantage in setting a short payback period is that the immediate years are probably more certain than the cash flows of the more distant years. Firms can therefore reduce exposure to risk by setting a short payback limit which covers the time period they can most accurately forecast. The disadvantage is that one arbitrary time limit is not flexible enough to deal fairly with the complex cash flows of many projects. Consequently, profitable opportunities may be lost through lack of a more sophisticated appraisal of risk.

As an example, let us assume Hasty Limited sets a payback limit of three years in addition to requiring projects to achieve a minimum 20% DCF yield. Two investments A and B have an equal degree of uncertainty. The application of the above criteria means the acceptance of the less profitable project as Figure 5.1 illustrates.

Were Projects A and B to have unequal degrees of uncertainty then this would have to be taken into account. Even in this case the payback criterion is still not a good method to use as it does not quantify the degree of uncertainty. Discounted payback can be used instead of the more con-

Figure 5.1 Selection of less profitable project by payback criterion

	Project A £	Project B £
Year 0	− 10,000	− 10,000
1	+ 4,000	0
2	+ 4,000	+ 4,000
3	+ 4,000	+ 4,000
4	+ 4,000	+ 4,000
5	—	+ 4,000
6	—	+ 4,000
7	—	+ 4,000
8	—	+ 4,000
Payback period	$2^1/_2$ years	$3^1/_2$ years
DCF yield	22%	25%

ventional undiscounted payback. By discounting the cash flows at the required rate of return this automatically gives less weighting to the more distant cash flows. This is because they are multiplied by relatively small present value factors. Conversely, a higher weighting is given to the more immediate cash flows when multiplied by larger present value factors. Risk is thus allowed for in the discounting process as the more immediate and more certain cash flows get the highest weightings. However, both payback and discounted payback suffer from the disadvantages of setting an arbitrary time limit and not quantifying the likelihood of future events.

An alternative approach is to recognize that different kinds of investment carry different degrees of risk and should therefore be set different target rates of return. This forms the basis of the next method.

Risk premium

All projects should satisfy the criterion of yielding a return at least equal to the cost of capital. By achieving a lower return a firm is not able to adequately reward the providers of capital. We can add an extra discount rate, called a 'risk premium', to the basic cost of capital so setting different target rates of return for different categories of investment.

The 'risk premium' may vary according to the risk category of the investment under review and is based on a subjective assessment of the risks involved. Past experience with similar projects can be useful in this context. The following hypothetical example illustrates this approach:

Figure 5.2 Varying the target rate of return for different risk categories of investments

Risk category	*Example*	*Cost of capital*	*Risk premium*	*Target rate of return*
No risk	Investment in govt securities	15%	Nil	15%
Low risk	Cost saving – existing technology	15%	3%	18%
Medium risk	Expansion – new markets	15%	10%	25%
High risk	Expansion – new markets and new technology	15%	20%	35%

Ideally firms should attempt to marry the risk premium to the cost of risk finance. In practice investors demand a higher return on more risky investments than on less risky ones. By using the 'risk premium' approach firms are giving recognition in their individual investments to what investors themselves practise when investing in individual companies. The difficulties in this approach are to ascertain what investors expect and also to express in one 'risk premium' all the possible uncertain future events.

Both the payback and risk premium methods express future events in one set of cash flows. Subsequent methods take the view that, because of uncertainty, more than one set of future cash flows is possible and that the analysis of risk should recognize this fact.

Pessimistic and optimistic forecasts

Instead of pinning all their faith on the DCF yield resulting from the expected cash flows, managers sometimes prepare two further sets of cash flows based on different assumptions. At one extreme will be the combination of the pessimistic assumptions. This will assume highest capital cost, shortest life, lowest sales volume and price, highest operating cost and the like. The DCF yield prepared from this data will be the lowest return envisaged.

At the other extreme will be the cash flows resulting from everything being favourable at the same time. This situation will incorporate the lowest possible capital cost, longest life, highest sales volume and price, lowest running cost and so on. The resultant DCF yield will be the highest possible return that could be achieved. In effect the pessimistic and optimistic forecasts set the outer limits, or parameters, within which we would expect to find the actual DCF yield.

To illustrate this approach let us suppose Unsure Limited requires a DCF yield of 20% on any project. A manager has prepared three sets of yearly cash flows for each of three projects A, B and C based on pessimistic, expected and optimistic assumptions. He has calculated the DCF yields as follows:

Figure 5.3 *DCF yields based on pessimistic, expected and optimistic forecasts of net cash flows*

	Pessimistic	*Expected*	*Optimistic*
Project A	22%	27%	40%
Project B	– 12%	12%	21%
Project C	– 3%	20%	40%

Project A will be approved as it satisfies the 20% required return in all conceivable circumstances. It is very unlikely that Project B will be approved, however, as only in the most optimistic circumstances will the 20% criterion just be satisfied. The whole balance of expectation on this second project weighs against its acceptance. Project C puts the decision-taking manager in the difficult position of an arbiter. He has to balance the possible loss against the possible high rate of return of 40%. The main drawback of this method is now apparent. It does not quantify the degree of optimism or pessimism assumed in the estimated cash flows, nor say how likely any of the three events are to occur. If either of the two extreme conditions are very unlikely to occur, managers should not pay them too much attention in their decision taking. In practice there will be many more combinations of possible events than the three mentioned above. We now want to examine how the DCF yield method can be adapted to give real help to managers in this more complex situation.

Sensitivity analysis

An alternative approach to relying on specific estimates of cash flows is to test how sensitive the DCF yield is to variations in any one cash flow item. For example, we can test the effect on the rate of return of a shorter or longer life than that expected. This is achieved by recalculating the DCF yield for sets of cash flows based on lives varying from the most pessimistic to the most optimistic assumption. A similar process can be repeated in turn for each uncertain element in the cash flows, holding all other data constant at its expected value. In this way we can separately examine possible variations in capital cost, life, sales volume, selling price, operating cost, tax, inflation, disposal value or any other uncertain item.

Let us take as an example a quotation of £80,000 which a firm has received for the insulation of its buildings. The justification for this investment is the expected energy saving valued at £17,600 for each of the next ten years. This equates to a DCF yield of 18%. There are, however, two possible uncertainties on this project. Savings in energy may be more or less than £17,600 each year and the life of the building may not exactly equal ten years. The sensitivity test in Figure 5.4 shows how responsive the DCF yield is to variations in either of these estimates whilst holding the other data constant.

There are a number of conclusions we can draw from this analysis. The DCF yield is little changed by any increase in the life of the buildings after ten years. From this time on, the rate of return responds increasingly slowly to peak at 22%. Therefore a shorter life than the expected ten years

Figure 5.4 Sensitivity tests on life of building and annual savings

Life of building	DCF yield (based on £17,600 saving)	Annual saving	DCF yield (based on 10 year life)
1-4 Years	Negative	£11,600	7%
6 Years	9%	£13,600	11%
8 Years	15%	£15,600	15%
10 Years	18%	£17,600	18%
12 Years	19%	£19,600	21%
14 Years	20%	£21,600	24%
50 Years	22%	£23,600	27%

will be significant, but any longer life will have little effect. In contrast the DCF yield is more responsive to fluctuations in the value of the yearly savings. If the £11,600 and £23,600 values represent the respective extremes of pessimism and optimism the project is profitable at all values of savings. Whether the investment is profitable enough to be viable depends on where this firm sets its target rate of return.

Managers will find this approach useful in a number of ways. The difficulty of making precise estimates can be avoided where a project is seen to be viable within the whole range of expected cash flows. It is usually easier to say whether a certain value will be reached than to quote one specific estimated value. Next, the key variables making up the cash flows can be identified as those which most influence the DCF yield. Projects can be re-examined to see if changes in working practices might make the DCF yield less responsive to variations in such key factors. Once a project is under way managers' attention can also be concentrated on those key factors which have been identified as critical to its profitability.

Research in recent years has demonstrated that the majority of firms do not allow for risk in this way. It is not suggested that all projects, large and small, should be sensitivity tested. Where a project is going to use up a significant portion of a firm's capital resources, however, it should be thoroughly sifted and analysed. For a firm with £1 m capital a project costing £20,000 or more may count as significant, whilst for a large firm the same proportion (2%) may serve as a useful, if somewhat arbitrary, yardstick.

One reason why managers baulk at this extra testing of a project's viability relates to the numerous calculations required. Fortunately computer programmes are available (or can be specially written) to cope with this aspect of financial modelling. Although the example in Figure 5.4 can be solved manually, more complex projects dealing with after-tax cash flows on revenue earning schemes would be extremely tedious. In this age of microcomputers even small companies can benefit from the technological advances of the 1970s and 1980s.

Sensitivity testing is a more useful and reliable measure of uncertainty than some of the earlier methods discussed. It is itself capable of further refinement and this relates to the likelihood of the different events occurring. Referring again to the example in Figure 5.4 it should not be assumed that the extreme savings of £11,600 and £23,600 will have an equal chance of taking place. Nor should we assume that either event is as likely to occur as the expected saving of £17,600 which has been calculated from a technical assessment of the saving in energy costs. Firms can benefit even more by introducing to their analysis the likelihood or probability of events taking place. Like many tasks that are worth doing, assessing probabilities may not be easy and is essentially only the subjective judgement of the manager concerned. It is a way of using a manager's experience to quantify the likelihood of a particular cash flow occurring.

Probability

Let us assume the manager in charge of the energy saving project outlined in Figure 5.4 has been asked to say how likely it is the energy savings will turn out to be £17,600 a year. His response is a one-in-three chance or a probability factor of 0.33, if 1.0 is regarded as certainty. When asked to repeat this process for each of the six other possible values of savings he allocates probability factors as in Figure 5.5 below. These factors weigh more heavily on the pessimistic side, indicating the manager's opinion that the annual savings are more likely to be less than the expected £17,600 value than to exceed it. If we take the probability factor for each value of saving and multiply it by the relevant DCF yield we can find the weighted average DCF yield for the project as follows:

Figure 5.5 Calculation of the weighted average DCF yield

Annual saving	*Probability factor*	*DCF yield*	*DCF yield × weight*	
£11,600	.05	7%	0.35%	
£13,600	.15	11%	1.65%	
£15,600	.25	15%	3.75%	
£17,600	.33	18%	5.94%	
£19,600	.15	21%	3.15%	
£21,600	.05	24%	1.20%	
£23,600	.02	27%	0.54%	
	1.00		16.58%	= weighted average DCF yield

The weighted average DCF yield turns out to be 16.58% which is slightly lower than the 18% return based on the original expected saving of £17,600 each year. This is to be expected as the probabilities were biased on the pessimistic side. It is possible to think of the dispersion of the possible savings value as an indication of risk. If the expected savings were still £17,600, but the extreme limits envisaged were only £15,600 and £19,600 respectively, then this latter situation is less risky than the former. We could use the 'standard deviation' as a measure of dispersion and therefore of risk but complications arise in some applications so this method is not pursued here.

On a more complex project like an expansion scheme to sell a new product we can apply probability factors to each constituent item making up the cash flows. The number of combinations of possible events will be enormous as any devotee of football pools will testify. If we combine, say, a range of seven possible capital costs with a range of seven possible annual profits over a range of seven possible lives we end up with 343 possible combinations. To manually calculate the weighted average DCF yield for all these possible outcomes would be an awesome task.

Fortunately computers can solve in a minute or two what humans take weeks to complete. Computer manufacturers have standard programmes for this kind of application. In this case the range of each cash flow item together with the respective probability of each value in the range is fed into the computer. A print-out is then obtained which in effect graphs the DCF yields against the cumulative frequency as in Figure 5.6 below. It is a risk profile showing the range of possible rates of return and the probability of their occurrence.

Figure 5.6 Typical risk profile of a project

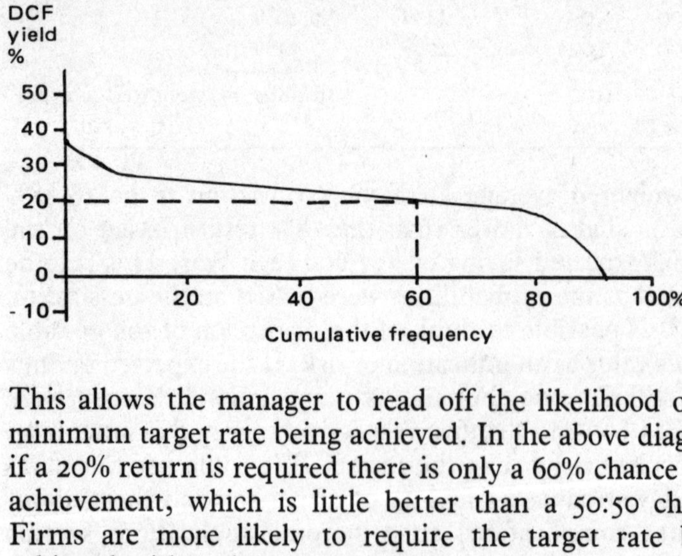

This allows the manager to read off the likelihood of the minimum target rate being achieved. In the above diagram, if a 20% return is required there is only a 60% chance of its achievement, which is little better than a 50:50 chance. Firms are more likely to require the target rate being achieved with at least a 90% level of confidence or thereabouts. Thus two criteria are being used to judge a project's viability – a minimum weighted average rate of return and a satisfactory level of confidence in it being achieved. Case Study No. 4 illustrates this approach for a property developer, when a range of possible rents are combined with different capital costs of the development. The number of combinations is kept small to allow the calculations to be performed manually.

Having introduced the idea of using probability in appraisals we can now look at a technique which incorporates it in a visual expression of the benefits arising from alternative courses of action.

Decision trees

Sometimes managers are faced with a choice between alternative courses of action with the possibility of further alternative courses of action in later years depending on which original choice was made. A technique known as a 'decision tree' is used to set out all possible alternatives and to show the further alternatives they lead to in future years. The analogy with a tree comes from the nodes and branches. At each node there is a choice of brances. Each branch leads to a further node at which another choice of branches is made and so on until all possible outcomes are exhausted.

If the nodes represent decision points for investment and the branches are quantified for the benefits gained, we can attach probability factors to each branch to quantify the expected monetary value of each alternative event. Managers should therefore choose the path which maximizes this money benefit.

Let us assume the manager of a research department is considering what to do about an ongoing project. He can either abandon it, keep the expenditure at the same level, or increase it substantially to improve the likelihood of success. Abandoning will result in costs of £20,000; maintaining the present level of activity will cost £50,000; doubling the present effort to improve the chances of success will cost £100,000. By the end of the year it will be known whether the project has succeeded or failed. Failure brings no further costs with it, whilst success would result in the sale of know-how for £300,000.

At the present level of research activity the success/failure ratio is put at 40%/60% but the enhanced effort would improve the prospects to about 80%/20%. All the above information can be expressed graphically in the form of a decision tree and the gains/losses from the various outcomes evaluated as follows:

Figure 5.7 Decision tree of alternative strategies on research project

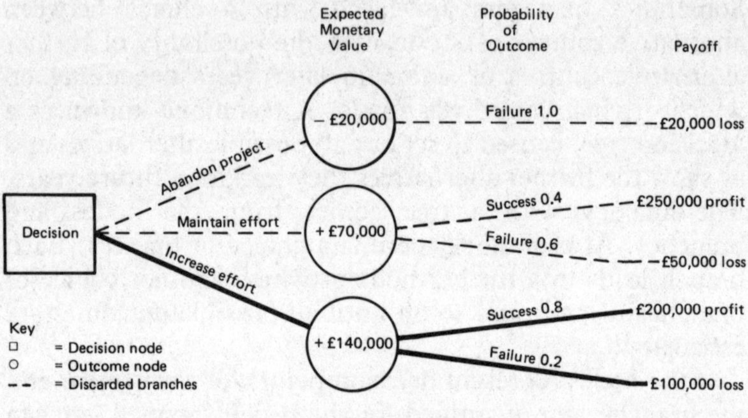

In the above example the three alternative courses of action are evaluated by netting off the probable gain against its respective cost. Taking the alternative to increase the research effort as an example, the expected monetary value of £140,000 = (0.8 × £200,000) – (0.2 × £100,000). This expected monetary value is the highest of the three alternatives and is therefore the preferred solution.

Of course this approach ignores the risk element other than that expressed by the probability factors. There is a 20% chance of failure on the recommended course of action. For a large firm with many projects this may be acceptable as the risk/reward ratio is very satisfactory. In a small firm the failure of this one project out of a small total may be catastrophic.

The above illustration of a decision tree did not include any subsequent decisions. Also, because of the short time span of only one year, the present value of money was ignored. It is when dealing with more complex situations that decision trees are most useful. They do not bring new information to bear on the decision but set it out in the most helpful way. The points of time at which decisions have to be made are clearly identified along with the different possible outcomes evaluated in money and probability terms. This enables the decision-making manager to choose the most desirable course of action based on the net present value of the weighted benefits less costs. Consider the following example.

Potential Limited are contemplating building a plant to make and sell a new product but are unsure of market demand. They can build and equip a large factory for £5.2 m but this would incur losses at the low level of demand. Alternatively, they can build a smaller factory now for £2.8 m capable of extension should demand turn out to be high. Market research has estimated sales potential at three levels (high, medium and low) with assigned probabilities to each level of sales at 60%, 30% and 10% respectively. Profits earned on these sales will differ between the two different-sized plants owing to the inability of the small plant to meet the high level of sales (without expansion) and the uneconomic operation of the large plant at the low level of sales. The expected annual profits have been kept constant for simplicity and their value for the next eight years is set out below:

Expected annual profits (pre-depreciation)

	Large plant	*Small plant*
High demand	£2.0 m	£0.9 m
Medium demand	£1.0 m	£0.7 m
Low demand	£0.4 m (loss)	£0.5 m

Assuming the small plant was constructed it will be able to cope with the low and medium levels of demand. If the high level of sales materializes it will be possible to extend the small plant at the end of Year 2 for a cost of £2.6 m after which annual profits will roughly equal those earned on the large plant.

These alternative courses of action and their net present value at the required rate of 20% can be represented on a decision tree as in Figure 5.8.

When interpreting a decision tree we start at the extreme right hand branches. The payoffs are 'rolled-back' to the previous decision point where a choice between alternatives takes place. Intermediate payoffs are rolled back to their previous decision point until one eventually reaches the original decision point. This first decision is dependent on which route through the branches maximizes the net present value benefit. In complex situations many decision points exist and the tree diagrams are quite involved, unlike Figure 5.8 which only includes two decision points.

In that example the second decision concerns the choice whether to expand the small scale plant after two years or not. On the current forecasts of demand and the likelihood of occurrence it does not appear worthwhile. The NPV surplus of £1.57 m is less than the £1.85 m obtained from running the small plant at its original size for a further six years. This preferred solution rolls back to influence the original decision to build the small plant because the NPV surplus of £0.88 m exceeds the £0.40 m surplus obtained from building the large plant.

Conclusions

It is unrealistic to assume that there will be one certain set of net cash flows on a project apart from exceptional cases. The consequence of more than one set of cash flows being possible means we should allow for this when assessing the profitability of an investment. Relatively crude techniques like payback, risk premium and optimistic/pessimistic forecasts can be used, but projects absorbing a significant amount of a firm's capital demand more sophisticated treatment.

The DCF yield or NPV methods can both be used to test how sensitive they are to variations in any one key variable

Figure 5.8 Decision tree of expansion project

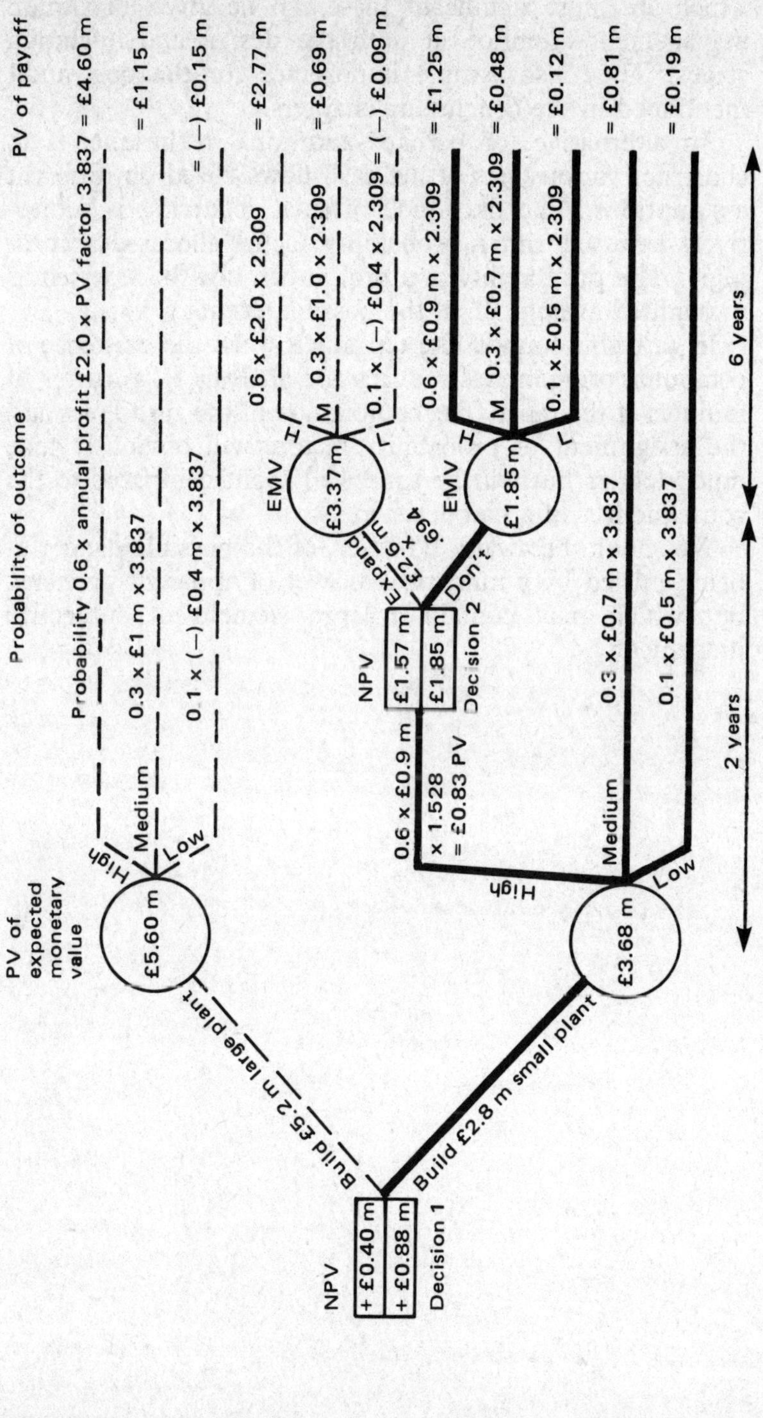

in the cash flows. Having identified the items of cash flow which are most significant these can be given maximum management attention at both the design and operation stages. They also assume importance for the post audit mentioned in the concluding chapters.

An alternative, or perhaps additional technique, is to construct various sets of net cash flows based on different assumptions. The likelihood of each occurring is subjectively assessed and a probability factor allocated accordingly. The profitability of a project can now be assessed as a weighted average of all the possible events.

In case this sounds like too much work the existence of computer programmes reduces the analysis to a matter of minutes at the most. The compilation of the cash flows and the assignment of probability factors will obviously take much longer but will be time well spent compared to the consequences of a bad decision.

We should be aware, however, of the possible danger of being misled by a numerical answer of apparent precision but which may contain a large element of subjective judgement.

6 What about inflation?

Unfortunately inflation is like the poor – always with us. Economic historians can point to times past when the value of money actually increased but these have been short-lived. In the present inflationary era we need to be able to distinguish between the apparent return on an investment and its real return after allowing for inflation.

This chapter first examines some of the broader issues of inflation accounting before homing in on how to deal with it on specific project appraisals.

Inflation has been present in the UK, as in the world economy, throughout the whole post-war period. When the rate of inflation was at a mild rate of less than 5% per annum, accountants along with others largely ignored its existence when preparing the annual accounting statements of profit and loss account and balance sheet. Over a number of years, however, even a modest rate of inflation like 5% per annum has a dramatic effect on the value of possessions (assets) of a firm. Even more important is the effect on the replacement cost of such assets when they eventually wear out and have to be renewed.

The basic problems presented by inflation when preparing the annual accounting statements are that profits are overstated in the profit and loss account and asset values are understated in the balance sheet. This leads to an incorrect assessment of the return earned on capital invested in the business and makes real performance hard to measure. In terms of the day-to-day running of the business there is also the danger that current selling prices may not reflect the up-to-date costs of stock and asset replacements. If this is the case cash earned by the business may often be insufficient to pay taxes, reward investors and finance these higher replacement costs of stock and plant. Very often it is the latter which suffers and the firm reinvests too little, either to finance inflation or to allow real growth.

In the 1970s when the rate of inflation in the UK rose into double figures, and by the mid 70s threatened to turn us into a banana republic, the professional accountancy bodies together with government-appointed committees finally agreed on the following system of inflation accounting.

Inflation accounting

More properly inflation accounting is called 'current cost accounting' and the specific procedure for accountants to follow is set out in Statement of Standard Accounting Practice No. 16 entitled *Current Cost Accounting*. This Statement requires companies listed on the Stock Exchange to clarify the effects of inflation on both the profit earned in the year and on the values of assets held at the year end. Usually this is done by the company producing supplementary statements to the original profit and loss account and balance sheet statements which are prepared on the basis of the original cost of the items, i.e. on 'historic cost' accounting principles.

The supplementary profit and loss account statement opposite contains the following adjustments to the 'historic cost' profit to arrive at the real profit attributable to the owners.

Additionally a supplementary balance sheet is prepared to show the up-to-date financial position of the company at the end of its accounting year. A balance sheet is so called because it reflects two aspects of the same money. First, who provided the company with money (capital) and, second, what assets that money was spent on. Therefore if because of inflation the assets are revalued in present day £s, a similar increase in value must be shown in the owners' capital. In this way the balance sheet remains in balance and also expresses values in £s of present-day purchasing power.

Generally speaking in most industries these supplementary statements show the real return on investment to be

		£000s
Profit as in 'historic cost' profit and loss account		1,000
Deduct: (a) Depreciation adjustment being the extra cost of depreciation calculated on the replacement cost of assets instead of their original cost	200	
(b) Cost of sales adjustment being the extra cash needed to replace stocks at prices ruling at the time of sale	300	
(c) Monetary working capital adjustment being the additional cash needed to give credit to customers for the value of goods which have cost more to produce	100	600
		400
Add back: The proportion of the above adjustments (a), (b) and (c) not required to be borne by the owners if part of the firm's capital is borrowed (assumed 50% in this example)		300
= *Real profit earned for owners*		700

much less, perhaps by one third on average, than what it appears to be when based on the figures in the historic cost statements.

There is not much evidence at the time of writing that company managers, investors, employees and possibly even accountants understand all the ramifications of these adjustments. The effects of inflation on pricing policy, working capital requirements, corporation tax assessments, dividend policy, the cost of capital and wage claims are complex and not easily understood. The tendency is for companies, unions and the financial press to concentrate on the well-known misleading figures and treat the recent more accurate information like bad news and simply ignore it.

Managers should be aware that inflation also increases the cost of capital. Interest rates on borrowed capital are partly influenced by the rate of inflation but more so by government action to contain it. Shareholders expect partial if not complete protection of their dividend income from the ravages of inflation. As the required or target rate of return must reflect these inflationary expectations then the conclusion must be that we should not invest in projects that do not meet this inflated minimum rate of return. To do otherwise will not lead to the real growth of the firm but the opposite, and may risk its long term survival. Having looked at all the general problems caused by inflation it is now time to look more specifically at the effects of inflation on a single project's profitability.

Effects of inflation on project appraisals

Up to this point the investment appraisal techniques discussed have implicitly ignored the existence of inflation and its effects on the future cash flows of projects being appraised. It would be a happier world for managers if this absence of inflation could be justified. Unfortunately, inflation exists in the real world, and although the rate of inflation may fluctuate from year to year, few pundits are forecasting its complete demise.

Inflation brings additional problems to project appraisals. It increases the uncertainty and makes more difficult the estimation of the future cash flows including sales revenue, operating costs and working capital requirements. As we have seen it also influences the required rate of return through its effects on the cost of capital.

In the context of investment appraisals it means that *two aspects* of the value of money must be considered. The *time value* of money has already been catered for by the use of present value factors which deduct interest for the time elapsed when waiting for future cash receipts. The other aspect is the change in the *value of money* itself, not because of the time lapse, but because the inflationary process decreases its purchasing power.

Real and nominal rates of return

When describing how to allow for inflation in investment appraisals, and cope with both these aspects, it is useful first to distinguish between the *real* rate of return on a project and its *nominal* rate of return. A simple example may clarify this difference between real and nominal rates of return:

Suppose an investor receives an income of £100 p.a. on an investment of £1,000 then his nominal rate of return is 10%. If inflation is zero then his real rate of return will also be 10%. If, however, inflation is running at 6% per annum then his real rate of return is approximately the nominal rate minus the rate of inflation which leaves only 4%.* Again, if inflation is running at 15% per annum then his nominal rate of return of 10% is swamped by inflation and he gets a negative real rate of return of about 5%. This experience has been all too vivid for small investors in the 1970s when the rate of inflation has frequently exceeded the rate of interest received on bank or building society deposits or other similar investments.

Turning to an industrial context a company's return on investment is the annual after-tax profit expressed as a percentage of the capital employed in the business. This is a nominal rate of return. The real return on investment will be this nominal return less the rate of inflation and it should be recognized that the real rate of return for British industry generally has been less than 5% in many recent years.

The real and nominal rates of return referred to here for the whole company are not strictly correct because the concept of profit is not identical with that of cash flow. This is because profit ignores the timing of cash receipts and payments and can arise when cash is not even received. It

* Real rate of return 0.04 (4%)

$$= \left(\frac{\text{nominal rate of return } 1.10}{\text{rate of inflation } 1.06}\right) - 1$$

or Nominal rate of return = 0.10 (10%)

$$\left(\underset{1.04}{\text{real rate of return}} \times \underset{1.06}{\text{rate of inflation}}\right) - 1$$

is important to recognize that the company's one year return on investment is conceptually different from the whole life project return based on the timing of cash flows. It is far from uncommon for a wholly satisfactory project with a high estimated return to have an adverse effect on the company profit and loss account particularly in the first year or two. This is because the initial investment costs show as depreciation and interest charges before revenue starts to flow and profits are earned.

In the case of individual project appraisals the nominal rate of return is the apparent DCF yield found when discounting future cash flows that have been inflated to take account of anticipated inflation. The real rate of return on such a project however is this nominal rate of return minus the rate of inflation. If future cash flows on a project have been expressed in the constant value of Year 0 purchasing power then the solution DCF yield is the *real* rate of return.

The following chapter further discusses real versus nominal rates of return and also explains how part of the effects of inflation are borne by the providers of loan capital and are not therefore totally borne by the owners of a company.

Quantifying the effects of inflation

At appraisal time managers are faced with the choice whether to express future cash flows at their inflated values and find the *nominal* rate of return or alternatively to express them in the constant purchasing power as at Year 0 and find the *real* rate of return. What influences managers as to which choice to make depends on how top management express the target rate of return and whether managers see the future cash flows keeping pace with inflation or not. Most firms will probably express the target rate of return in nominal rather than real terms. This is because the target rate is often based on the nominal costs of borrowing or the opportunity cost of alternative financial investments.

The effects of inflation can best be illustrated by a series of short simple examples all based on the same data but varied for different assumptions of the effects of inflation. The relevant information is an investment of £97,170 with a four year life generating sales revenue of £100,000 p.a. with labour, material, etc. costs of £70,000 p.a. to give a profit (before charging depreciation) of £30,000 p.a. Taxation and working capital are initially excluded for ease of illustration.

Figure 6.1 Calculation of the rate of return assuming zero inflation

Year	*Capital cost* £	*Sales revenue* £	*Labour, material, etc.* £	*Net cash flows* £	*PV factors @ 9%*	*Present value* £
0	− 97,170			− 97,170	1.000	− 97,170
1		+ 100,000	− 70,000	+ 30,000	.917	+ 27,510
2		+ 100,000	− 70,000	+ 30,000	.842	+ 25,260
3		+ 100,000	− 70,000	+ 30,000	.772	+ 23,160
4		+ 100,000	− 70,000	+ 30,000	.708	+ 21,240
					NPV	0

The *nominal* rate of return on this project is 9% which is also the *real* rate of return when inflation is zero.

If all cash flows on a project are affected equally by inflation, and at the same time, there is no effect on the real rate of profitability. On revenue–earning projects this assumes that selling prices rise at the same rate as costs without any time lag. In the case of cost-saving projects this assumes, justifiably in most cases, that the increased costs to be saved will keep pace with the general inflation rate. In both cases it is assumed no significant working capital is involved. When this assumption of keeping pace with inflation can be made then the firm can express the future cash flows in the constant purchasing power of Year 0 and discount to find the *real* rate of return. The nominal rate of return on such a project is this real rate plus the expected rate of inflation. The real rate of return may turn out to appear relatively low but it should be looked at in terms of opportunity cost as few financial investments in recent years have yielded a positive real rate of return at all. The opportunity cost referred to here is the cost of foregoing the next best use of company finance. Other uses of finance could be repaying loans or overdrafts, investing in government stocks or other financial securities or even paying larger dividends to shareholders.

When the zero inflation assumption is relaxed there are only two possible outcomes. Either the cash flows on the project will keep pace with inflation or they will not. Taking the former case first it is now assumed that inflation proceeds at 10% p.a. on a compound basis and that both costs and revenues increase at the same pace.

Figure 6.2 Calculation of the rate of return assuming 10% p.a. inflation on all cash flows

Year	*Capital cost* £	*Sales revenue* £	*Labour, materials, etc.* £	*Net cash flows* £	*PV factors @ 20%*	*Present value* £
0	− 97,170			− 97,170	1.000	− 97,170
1		+ 110,000	− 77,000	+ 33,000	.833	+ 27,489
2		+ 121,000	− 84,700	+ 36,300	.694	+ 25,192
3		+ 133,100	− 93,170	+ 39,930	.579	+ 23,119
4		+ 146,410	− 102,487	+ 43,923	.482	+ 21,171
					NPV −	£199

The *nominal* rate of return on this same project is now 20% which is equivalent to a *real* rate of return of 9% as found in Figure 6.1.

The above assumption of the future cash flows keeping pace with inflation is shown not to affect the real rate of profitability. If this was always the case then inflation would not be a problem in project appraisals.

An alternative approach is sometimes used and involves a double discounting exercise. The inflated net cash flows in Figure 6.2 can be discounted by 10% PV factors to bring them back to constant Year 0 purchasing power. This would result in the net cash flows as shown in Figure 6.1 which are then discounted to find the real rate of return is still 9%.

The other possible outcome is that the cash flows on the project do not keep pace with inflation. Some of the costs and revenues may be inflating at different rates to others on the same project and some cash flows like taxation do not inflate at all. This lack of synchronization has been the experience in the UK when, for example, wages have tended over the years to outstrip prices in general. In this situation the manager has to inflate each component cash flow separately to build up the future annual net cash flows. These future cash flows can then be discounted to find the nominal rate of return from which the real rate of return can be deduced if required.

To illustrate this situation it is now assumed that the general rate of inflation is 10% p.a. and that costs increase at that same rate whilst sales revenue increases only by 7% p.a.:

Figure 6.3 Calculation of the rate of return with differential inflation on costs and revenues

Year	*Capital cost* £	*Sales revenue* £	*Labour, materials, etc.* £	*Net cash flows* £	*PV factors @ 8%*	*Present value* £
0	− 97,170			− 97,170	1.000	− 97,170
1		+ 107,000	− 77,000	+ 30,000	.926	+ 27,780
2		+ 114,490	− 84,700	+ 29,790	.857	+ 25,530
3		+ 122,500	− 93,170	+ 29,330	.794	+ 23,288
4		+ 131,080	− 102,487	+ 28,593	.735	+ 21,016
					NPV +	£444

The nominal rate of return on this project is about 8% which is equivalent to a *real* rate of return of about −2% when inflation is 10%.

Clearly the effect of this differential inflation on revenue and costs has had a dramatic effect on profitability. What might have seemed to be just a marginal slippage of sales revenue against costs more than halved the nominal rate of return from 20% to 8%. It also completely eliminated the real rate of return which was as high as 9% when sales revenue was assumed to keep pace with inflation.

On revenue-earning projects the greater the differential effect, either by costs increasing faster than revenue or some costs increasing faster than general inflation, then the greater the effect on real profitability. Just imagine the effect on the real rate of return of sales held constant by a fixed price contract that had not included an allowance for inflation when the contract was negotiated!

As an example of this situation let us now assume that costs are inflating at the general rate of 10% p.a. whilst sales revenue is held constant on a fixed price contract:

Figure 6.4 *Calculation of the rate of return assuming 10% p.a. general inflation and sales on a fixed price contract*

Year	*Capital cost* £	*Sales revenue* £	*Labour, materials, etc.* £	*Net cash flows* £
0	− 97,170			− 97,170
1		+ 100,000	− 77,000	+ 23,000
2		+ 100,000	− 84,700	+ 15,300
3		+ 100,000	− 93,170	+ 6,830
4		+ 100,000	− 102,487	− 2,487
				− £54,527

In this case the cash inflows do not recover the original investment resulting in a total loss of £54,527. This is before any discounting is done to take account of the time value and inflation. In other words the nominal rate of return is negative and the real rate of return even more so.

The effects of inflation on working capital

Inflation creates tremendous cash flow problems for many firms. Not only is the replacement cost of fixed assets increased but, usually more important, extra cash is needed each and every year to finance the increased money value of working capital. This extra cash is needed each year to finance the increased labour, material and overhead costs which are normally paid for long before the money comes in from customers. Free credit from suppliers also increases in money value with inflation and this helps to finance the increase in a firm's own working capital items of stocks and debtors. The silly situation can be reached whereby a firm can produce and sell less during a recession but still need more cash for its working capital because the rate of inflation on its costs has exceeded the decrease in volume of goods produced.

The basic example used in Figure 6.1 assumed an investment of £97,170 excluding working capital. It would be more realistic to suppose that some additional investment is needed for working capital, i.e. to finance stocks and give credit to customers. Assuming stock levels are financed by creditors this leaves debtors to be financed by the firm itself. With a sales level of £100,000 we can assume 20% of this figure might represent the maximum amount of money owed by customers at any one time. Therefore the working capital required at the start of the project will be £20,000 and will remain at this figure over the whole life of the project *provided* sales volume and selling prices remain constant.

We also assumed a constant volume of sales in our basic model so that any increased sales value is caused by increased selling prices. Ignoring other factors we will attribute these sales value increases to the firm keeping pace with its inflated costs. What effect has this on the working capital requirements of the firm? The £20,000 working capital that was adequate with zero inflation will now need to be topped up each year. This is because the credit given to customers represents the increasing costs of labour, materials and overheads already paid for by the firm. Using the assumption of 10% per annum inflation with all cash flows keeping pace as in Figure 6.2 this would mean the cash outflows in Figure 6.5 would be required for extra working capital.

Over the life of this short project nearly 50% more cash is needed for working capital than would be the case if inflation did not exist and £20,000 sufficed. Obviously the greater the rate of inflation and the longer the life of the project the greater this extra cash requirement will be.

Apart from the above cash flow problem the other effect will be on the profitability of the project. Interest will have to be paid or forgone on the extra money tied up in working capital each year. Therefore the rate of return on this project will be reduced compared with the same project when inflation did not exist.

Figure 6.5 Calculation of working capital requirements assuming inflation at 10% p.a.

	Sales level for coming year	*Total working capital required* (assumed to equal 20% of sales)	*Change in working capital required increase (decrease)*
	£	£	£
Year 0	110,000	22,000	22,000
1	121,000	24,200	2,200
2	133,100	26,620	2,420
3	146,410	29,282	2,662
4	—	—	(29,282)

Our earlier assumption that the real return on a project is not affected by inflation, provided sales revenue keeps pace with inflation, should now be modified. Although sales revenue may keep pace, the cash flows do not, because extra working capital is required each year.

The effects of inflation on taxation

We considered in Chapter 4 how two aspects of taxation are built into the net cash flows of a project. On the one hand companies make tax payments based on the previous year's profit whilst on the other the size of that taxable profit is reduced by capital allowances on new investment and stock relief on inflated stock values. What effects has inflation on these tax transactions? The answer, fortunately, is a not very adverse effect except when capital allowances cannot immediately be offset against profits.

Tax payments are based on the adjusted historic cost profit and no additional tax is levied by the Inland Revenue to compensate for the normal time lag of about one year. The payment of tax by companies is therefore favourably affected by inflation as it reduces the *real* cost of the payments.

In the case of 100% capital allowances on plant and

machinery these reduce the size of the taxable profits and their benefit is reduced in real value by the same time lag as the tax payment. When capital allowances cannot immediately be offset against profits this will have a more adverse effect. This can occur either when profits for the whole firm are insufficient to claim the valuable capital allowance immediately, or when the capital allowance itself is claimable over a number of years as in the case of eligible buildings. In these situations the capital allowance is of reduced value because reduced tax payments in later years are not as valuable as one large reduced tax payment in a year or two's time. The position is the same regarding stock relief. Because tax payments are reduced by the amount of stock relief granted, the real benefit is reduced by the time lag from the start of the company year to the date of payment of mainstream tax.

Case Study No. 3 deals with an expansion project and demonstrates the combined effects of inflation and taxation.

Estimating future inflation

The previous discussions on inflating future cash flows may have sounded all too easy to do in principle but do we really need to try to estimate inflation over the next few years? There are a few ways we can tackle this question. In some cases there is no need to estimate the effects of inflation at all if the assumption that cash flows will keep pace with inflation can realistically be made. This applies when selling price can be immediately adjusted to recover increased costs without loss of volume, or, on cost saving schemes, where the costs to be saved would normally keep in step with inflation. This latter situation of cost savings keeping pace would be a valid assumption in many cases.

This leaves projects with a differential effect or with a significant working capital requirement. Very few managers would want to forecast inflation rates more than one year ahead but nearly all projects are going to last more than one year. It would be valid to estimate inflation at different rates in different years but few managers could attempt such sophistications. What we can do on important projects is to run sensitivity tests on different assumptions of inflation rates to see the effect on the nominal rate of return. This turns the problem the other way around. Instead of having to forecast future inflation rates we can calculate what rate of inflation would make a project no longer viable. We can then use our judgement to decide whether such rate(s) of inflation are likely to occur. In effect inflation is just another of those uncertainties surrounding future events and should be treated as such.

Large terminal values

When thinking personally about the effects of inflation one tends to think of house or other property values. These assets have tended at least to keep pace and often to exceed the general rate of inflation. There is a danger that some commercial and industrial projects may be thought to be viable on the strength of a large rise in the residual value of an asset rather than on the profits earned from the basic trading activity.

A case in point may arise in the brewing industry when an investment to refurbish a public house may appear to be justified on the grounds of increased trade and an enhanced terminal property value. The danger here is that the increased trade may not justify the investment in the refurbishing cost but the enhanced property value might. Breweries facing this situation should ask themselves whether they are operating in the brewing industry or in property development. The refurbishing cost should be justified by the extra profits from the increased trade alone during the expected life of the refurbishing, leaving out property values. This is because when investments are being appraised we are concerned only with the extra (or incremental) cash flows. Those cash flows which do not result from the investment decision should be ignored. Case Study No. 5 illustrates this aspect of a large inflated terminal value.

Conclusions

In the real world the effects of inflation on a project's viability must be considered. The target rate of return should be looked at each year in the light of inflationary expectations. It will normally be expressed as a nominal rate of return.

Cash flows on a project that can be expected to keep pace with inflation can be expressed in Year 0 value £s and the resultant real DCF yield modified to a nominal rate by adding the rate of inflation.

When cash flows on a project are not expected to synchronize with inflation generally they can be inflated at the estimated rate(s) and discounted to find the nominal DCF yield. This can then be compared with the nominal target rate of return.

An alternative approach to estimating future inflation rates is to turn the problem round and test how sensitive the DCF yield is to various possible inflation rates. This will then highlight at what inflation rate a project becomes no longer viable and managers can use their judgement as to whether such events are likely to occur.

7 How much should a project earn?

Capital is not free. The owners of firms and financial institutions require a return on their investment in the company. In turn the company must earn a return on projects at least equal to this cost of capital. To do otherwise will not satisfy the providers of that capital and make the raising of future capital more difficult.

Previous chapters have assumed various discount rates for firms when appraising projects. We now need to examine how firms should set the minimum required rate of return on new investments. This minimum rate serves as the discount rate used in NPV calculations or the target rate for comparison with the DCF yield on each project.

Firms have two main sources of new capital for new investments. They can either borrow the money, usually from a financial institution, or they can obtain it from the owners. In this latter case new equity capital can be obtained in one of two ways. Companies occasionally sell new shares to existing shareholders on a 'rights' issue. This may be unpopular as it tends to depress the existing share price on the Stock Exchange. The other way companies obtain new capital from the owners is by not paying out all the profits earned as dividends. By this means companies are assured of the extra capital they need and they save the expense of issuing new shares.

Most firms use a mix of borrowed and owners' capital and the relationship between the two is known as 'capital gearing'. A company is said to be highly geared when it has a large amount of borrowed capital relative to owners' capital. It is lowly geared when the proportion of borrowed capital is small. The relationship between these two sources of capital is also expressed by calculating each source as a proportion of the total capital. The following two situations illustrate different levels of gearing:

Figure 7.1 Example of high and low capital gearing

	(a) *Low gearing*	(b) *High gearing*
Owners' capital (share capital + retained profits)	90%	50%
Borrowed capital	10%	50%
Total capital	100%	100%

There is no one particular level of capital gearing that is regarded as satisfactory for all companies. Each firm is examined on its past record, future prospects and the security of the interest and capital repayments. In most industries the 50% borrowed capital indicated in Figure 7.1(b) would be regarded as very high, although much higher rates are not uncommon in the rather special case of property development.

It is possible to find examples of companies with no borrowed capital, resulting from a policy decision by management to finance growth internally from retained profits. Such companies eliminate the risks of defaulting on the loan or interest repayments, or having to reduce dividends to make interest payments when profits fall. On the other hand they miss the opportunity of increasing the return to shareholders by investing borrowed capital to earn more than the cost of the interest as Figure 7.2 shows.

When a company has no gearing the change in the profit results in the same proportionate change in the return on shareholders' funds. In the above nil gearing example doubled profits also double the return to the owners from 7.5% to 15%. The doubling of the same profit in the high gearing example more than doubles the return on ordinary shareholders' funds from 9% to 21%.

Most firms decide that a judicious amount of borrowed capital is beneficial and try to adhere to a target level of gearing over the years. It may be that in any one year the target is exceeded because conditions in the capital markets

Figure 7.2 Illustration of the effects of capital gearing

	Nil gearing (£000)	*High gearing* (£000)
Capital structures:		
Ordinary share capital	3,000	1,500
Retained profits	1,000	1,000
10% loan stock	—	1,500
	4,000	4,000
Profit of £600,000		
Profit	600	600
Interest	—	150
	600	450
Corporation tax at (say) 50%	300	225
Earned for ordinary shareholders	300	225
Return on ordinary shareholders' funds	7.5%	9.0%
Profit of £1,200,000		
Profit	1,200	1,200
Interest	—	150
	1,200	1,050
Corporation tax at (say) 50%	600	525
Earned for ordinary shareholders	600	525
Return on ordinary shareholders' funds	15.0%	21.0%

do not allow a particular kind of funding to take place. This can be redressed as soon as market conditions allow.

New projects must be financed by new capital, as opposed to existing capital which has already been spent on existing projects. We therefore need to look at the cost and the mix of new capital to calculate the required rate of return. Also we must bear in mind the effects of taxation and inflation on each type of capital as they differ in certain respects. We will first examine the cost of borrowed capital, then the cost of equity, and weight the different proportions to get an overall cost.

The cost of borrowed capital

The rate of interest which has to be paid on new loans to get them taken up by investors at par can be regarded as the cost of borrowed capital. Such rates of interest vary over time in sympathy with interest rates obtainable on alternative investments. They also vary slightly according to the size of the loan and the degree of risk attached to the particular firm.

An alternative approach can be used to find the current cost of borrowing for a firm which has existing quoted loans or debentures. If the fixed rate of interest on such loans is less than the current going rate, these securities will have a market price of less than the par value of the stock. This means investors will obtain an annual return from the interest payments and a capital gain on the eventual repayment of the stock at par.

Suppose X Limited has a 10% loan stock standing at £83 per £100 nominal value, repayable at par in five years time. An investor today is therefore willing to pay £83 for the right to receive £10 yearly interest for the next five years and his £100 back at the end of that time. We can approach this in the way we calculate the DCF yield for industrial investments to find the solution rate of interest at 15% as shown in Figure 7.3.

The DCF yield of 15% obtained by an investor buying the company's existing loan stock can be regarded as the current cost of interest on new loans issued at par. It represents the money or nominal cost of new loans, which is used to calculate the target rate of return in nominal terms, as discussed in Chapter 6. The real cost of loan capital will be significantly less as investors are not compensated for the fall in the value of their capital. This is the reason for the 'gearing adjustment' in the inflation-adjusted profit and

Figure 7.3 Calculation of the DCF yield on the investment of £83 in £100 of 10% loan stock repayable in five years' time

Year	*Cash flow* £	*PV factors at 15%*	*PV* £
0	− 83	1.000	− 83.00
1	+ 10	.870	+ 8.70
2	+ 10	.756	+ 7.56
3	+ 10	.658	+ 6.58
4	+ 10	.572	+ 5.72
5	+ 110	.497	+ 54.67
			+ £0.23

loss account. In recent years this real cost of loan capital has been negative after allowing for both inflation and the tax relief next mentioned.

Interest on loans, debentures and overdrafts is deductible from profits before calculating the corporation tax charge, whereas dividends are not. In effect tax relief is granted on interest payments which, with corporation tax at 52%, virtually halves the rate of interest. The following example illustrates this point:

Figure 7.4 Illustration of tax relief on interest payments

	Company A (no gearing)		*Company B* (50% gearing)
Shareholders funds	£10 m		£ 5 m
10% loan	—		£ 5 m
Total capital employed	£10 m		£10 m
Profit before tax and interest	£2,000,000		£2,000,000
Interest on loan	—		£ 500,000
Profit after interest	£2,000,000		£1,500,000
Corporation tax at (say) 50%	£1,000,000		£ 750,000
Tax saved		£250,000	

It can be seen that the above two companies with identical total capitals and annual profits do not pay the same tax charge. Company B which financed half of its capital requirement from a 10% loan saves £250,000 of the £500,000 interest cost through tax relief. The effective rate of tax on the loan is therefore only 5% (£0.25 m/£5.00 m × 100/1%). It is not surprising that firms find gearing attractive when they compare the after-tax cost of loans with the cost of equity capital!

The cost of equity capital

The equity of a company is its risk capital, embracing ordinary share capital and retained profits which can both be regarded as having the same cost. Companies retain profits to short circuit paying out all profits with one hand whilst asking shareholders to buy new shares with the other. There is clearly a saving in administrative costs and professional fees by retaining profits, so this alternative will be slightly cheaper in practice.

Put simply, the cost of equity is the return shareholders expect the company to earn on their money. It is their estimation, often not scientifically calculated, of the rate of return which will be obtained both from future dividends and an increased share value. Unfortunately, simple concepts are not always so easy to apply in practice and the cost of capital is a favourite battlefield for academics with no one agreed practical solution.

It is possible to calculate the cost of equity as the DCF yield achieved from the estimated future dividends and the increased share value at a future point of time. This corresponds to the approach used to calculate the cost of borrowed capital in Figure 7.3. An alternative approach is to take the current dividend yield for a company and add the expected annual growth. For example, Graham Limited currently pay a net dividend of 20p on each ordinary share which is quoted at £2 on the Stock Exchange. Growth of profits and dividends has averaged 15% over the last few years. The cost of equity for Graham Limited can be calculated as:

$$\text{cost of equity capital} = \frac{\text{current net dividend}}{\text{current market price}}\% + \text{growth rate}\%$$

$$= \left(\frac{20\text{p}}{£2} \times \frac{100}{1}\%\right) + 15\%$$

$$= 25\%$$

With this method dividends are assumed to grow in the future at the constant rate achieved by averaging the last few years' performance. This growth is best calculated from profits after tax, rather than dividends, as changes in company dividend policy or government controls over dividend payments can distort short term trends. No residual share price is included as it is assumed that dividend payments continue to perpetuity. The 25% cost of equity capital above is a nominal rate rather than a real rate of return to investors. It is an after-tax return as dividends are paid from taxed profits, unlike interest payments which are allowed against tax. Fortunately UK corporation tax is neutral between profits retained and profits paid out as dividends.

Another way to calculate the cost of equity is to calculate the real rate of return earned by investors on a wide portfolio of shares over a long period of years. Such analysis indicates an after-tax real return of considerably less than 10% in the booming 1950s and 60s. If used as a guide to performance in the 70s it is likely to prove over-optimistic. With inflation at 20% per annum in some years a real rate of return of, say, 8% equates to a nominal rate of 30% after corporation tax. Such returns are not widely available and investors may have had to settle for considerably less in periods of high inflation.

The above market-based approach assumes the same element of risk for one company as for the whole portfolio, whereas a more recent approach takes this into account. Known as the 'capital-asset pricing model', a particular company's share performance is measured against the whole market performance for a period of years. In both cases the risk-free return earned on short dated government securities is excluded so that the risk premium or discount against the market generally can be ascertained. The nominal cost of equity capital for any one company therefore comprises the after-tax risk-free return plus the market risk premium plus the company risk premium (or discount) against the market.

It is unlikely that all the above techniques will coincide but it is also unlikely that there will be very wide differences. We must always remember that a precise calculation will only really matter for marginal projects rather than the vast majority of schemes which are either more than marginally profitable, or totally unviable. Having decided on the cost of equity we can reassure ourselves by conducting a few simple tests. The cost of equity should be more than the pre-tax cost of borrowed capital because of the greater element of risk. Taken over only one year this does not appear to be the case as evidenced by the 'reverse yield gap' which measures the excess of the current fixed interest rate over the current dividend yield on shares. As dividends increase in future years whereas interest remains fixed, this results in the cost of equity exceeding the cost of borrowed capital when taken to perpetuity.

Another comparison we can make is to look at the shareholder's opportunity cost if he made alternative investments. If the cost of equity appears lower than the return achievable on other financial securities of equal or lesser risk, we should go back to the drawing board. Either the calculation of the cost of equity is incorrect or we cannot justify investing more equity capital to achieve a lower return than shareholders expect.

New projects are financed by a mix of borrowed capital and equity capital. Having determined their separate costs we now need to combine them together to calculate the weighted average cost of capital at the desired level of capital gearing.

Weighted average cost of capital

Let us assume Canny Limited attempt to keep their gearing ratio of borrowed capital to shareholders' funds in the proportion of 30:70. The nominal cost of new capital from these sources has been assessed at 18% and 22% respectively. We now need to take account of the tax relief on interest, the cost of each type of new capital, and the mix of types to calculate the overall cost as follows:

Figure 7.5 Calculation of the nominal weighted average cost of capital

Type of capital	Proportion		After-tax cost		Weighted cost
18% loan capital	0.3	×	9%	=	2.7%
Shareholders' funds	0.7	×	22%	=	15.4%
	1.0				18.1%

The resulting weighted average cost of 18% is the minimum rate at which Canny Limited will perform NPV calculations on any proposed investments. Similarly it is the minimum target with which to compare the nominal DCF yield on such projects. Any investment which is not expected to achieve an 18% return is not a viable proposition for this firm. When firms weight the cost of capital for risk by adding a risk premium, this may result in a substantially higher target being set for some projects.

New investments are financed from a pool of funds rather than from one particular source, except in the case of particularly large projects. This pool (see Figure 1.3) is composed primarily of borrowed and owners' capital together with depreciation and other retained profits. We can think of depreciation as retained profit for the specific purpose of helping to replace any assets that have worn out during the year. Such asset replacements allow those projects to continue to earn a return provided this is still satisfactory. When we appraise replacements we can use the current cost of capital to choose between alternative replacements and to decide when the replacement should take place.

Projects earning no return

In reality the minimum required rate of return may have to be set higher than the overall cost of capital because firms sometimes spend capital on projects which earn no rate of return at all.

Examples of this situation occur when firms provide sports facilities for their employees or when buildings have to be altered to comply with new fire regulations. The investment of capital in such projects means that the remaining capital has to earn a slightly higher return on revenue-earning projects to meet the overall cost of capital. If the proportion of such non-revenue-earning projects is 5% of the total, this will increase the above 18% weighted average cost of capital to about 19% overall.

Capital rationing

When firms have access to unlimited funds then any investment which is expected to achieve the required rate of return can proceed. Only projects whose NPV is negative, or whose DCF yield is less than the minimum required return, will be rejected. It does not matter whether we evaluate projects by their NPV or their DCF yield in this case as the only test of viability is whether they match the minimum required return.

Funds are not always in plentiful supply, however, and may be insufficient to allow all profitable projects to proceed. This occurs when the owners have already invested all their capital in the business and do not wish to borrow or dilute their ownership. Here their firms will grow at the pace dictated by the size of retained profits as this is the only source of finance for new projects. Small companies are often in this situation. Other companies may face a shortage of funds if they are already highly geared, or when market conditions do not allow the raising of new share capital at that time.

Faced with the constraint of a capital shortage a firm has to ration out the available funds on the most profitable projects. Now we face the same problem as we did in the case of mutually exclusive projects, namely that the projects with the highest DCF yield are not necessarily the ones to choose. For example, a 30% return for three years is not as good as a 29% return for a much longer period. Is the NPV method the answer? The size of the NPV surplus is used to choose between two or more mutually exclusive projects.

However, it should not be used for rationing purposes because the largest NPV may take a disproportionate amount of capital to achieve.

The best way to ration out scarce capital is to use the profitability index method previously mentioned in Chapter 2. This relates the NPV of all cash inflows to the NPV of the original investment. Viable projects will have an index number greater than 1.000 and the larger the index number the greater the return per £ of scarce capital outlay. Funds should therefore be allocated to projects starting with the highest profitability index then descending in rank order until the capital is exhausted.

To clarify this approach let us assume Farlon Limited has only £190,000 to invest with no access to further funds. It is faced with five possible investments all of which are viable at the 15% required rate of return but which have a total initial outlay of £390,000. The projects and their solutions are set out below:

Figure 7.6 Appraisal of projects in a capital rationing situation

	Project				
	A	B	C	D	E
Project life	2 yrs	5 yrs	5 yrs	4 yrs	5 yrs
Net cash flows (£)					
Year 0	− 100,000	− 120,000	− 50,000	− 90,000	− 30,000
1	+ 69,440	+ 38,400	+ 17,100	+ 36,100	+ 10,900
2	+ 69,440	+ 38,400	+ 17,100	+ 36,100	+ 10,900
3	—	+ 38,400	+ 17,100	+ 36,100	+ 10,900
4	—	+ 38,400	+ 17,100	+ 36,100	+ 10,900
5	—	+ 38,400	+ 17,100	—	+ 10,900
NPV @ 15%	+ 12,909	+ 8,717	+ 7,319	+ 13,066	+ 6,537
DCF yield	25%	18%	21%	22%	24%
Profitability index	1.129	1.073	1.146	1.145	1.218

According to which of the above three criteria is used, the ranking of the five projects will be in the order opposite. This firm has insufficient capital to undertake all five investments and therefore the ranking method is important as different rankings produce different total NPVs. Let us

Ranking method	*Ranking order*
NPV @ 15%	D, A, B, C, E
DCF yield	A, E, D, C, B
Profitability index	E, C, D, A, B

assume that none of the projects are mutually exclusive and that any project is divisible into fractions for ease of explanation. Farlon Limited will maximize the NPV surplus on its limited funds when it allocates the capital to projects by the size of the profitability index rather than the size of the NPV or DCF yield. This can be verified using the same five projects:

Figure 7.7 Comparison of NPVs using different ranking methods in a capital rationing situation

	Ranking by NPV			Ranking by DCF yield			Ranking by profitability index	
	Outlay	NPV		Outlay	NPV		Outlay	NPV
D	90,000	13,066	A	100,000	12,909	E	30,000	6,537
A	100,000	12,909	E	30,000	6,537	C	50,000	7,319
B	—	—	⅔D	60,000	8,711	D	90,000	13,066
C	—	—	C	—	—	⅕A	20,000	2,582
E	—	—	B	—	—	B	—	—
	190,000	25,975		190,000	28,157		190,000	29,504

The profitability index gives the combination of projects which yields the largest NPV surplus at the 15% required rate of return. The remaining two methods will never select a group of projects to yield a higher NPV than found by the profitability index but they may swop places with each other.

When firms face more than one constraint simultaneously, the problem of capital rationing becomes more difficult to solve manually. It is easily capable of solution by operational research techniques allied to computer use. For example, a firm may want to ration scarce capital over a number of available projects. It also requires that profits disclosed in the profit and loss account never fall below a certain figure during the build-up of the same investments. The combination of investments finally selected in this case must maximize the NPV consistent with earning the required level of profits to report to shareholders. These two objectives often conflict with each other in the short term due to investments not being immediately profitable although perfectly viable over their whole life.

Conclusions

Managers need to assess the cost of the mix of equity and borrowed capital in proportion to the desired gearing ratio. Tax relief on interest payments reduces the cost of borrowed capital *vis-à-vis* equity. The weighted average of all capital is expressed in nominal terms and should be adjusted yearly to reflect, if not fully compensate for, inflation. The resultant cost of capital should be increased to allow for non-revenue-earning projects. Firms using the risk premium approach will also load the cost of capital in line with their assessment of risk on each project. When insufficient capital is available it is rationed out to those projects with the highest profitability index.

8 What is life cycle costing?

Life cycle costing is a relatively new concept which attempts to optimize the cost of physical assets over their whole life. The choice of buildings or plant is often based solely on original capital costs without regard to subsequent operating costs, maintenance costs or replacement intervals. Life cycle costing brings together all the costs of ownership and operation over the whole life of an asset using the present value technique. It can therefore be used to evaluate trade-off situations, for example between a higher initial cost to save on future running costs, or between one asset and an alternative asset with different cost characteristics.

You will all have seen the following kind of advertisement: 'This washing machine is easily the cheapest on the market. It won't last!' The unintentional double meaning speaks volumes for the need to look at the total costs of the washing machine over its whole life, rather than just concentrate on the initial acquisition cost. In other words it is important to realize that the lowest purchase cost is not necessarily the lowest overall cost over the whole life of the asset. Higher maintenance costs and a shorter life may outweigh the higher acquisition cost of an alternative washing machine.

Most firms normally keep a record of assets acquired and somewhere else in their costing system keep details of the operating and maintenance costs of these same assets. What very few firms do is to put all this information together to monitor the cost of owning and using assets over their whole life. In other words few firms practise what is called 'life cycle costing'. This technique calls for the prediction of expected life cycle costs (LCC) for management decision-making purposes and the monitoring of actual

LCC to modify decisions previously made and to provide data for future decisions. It is therefore concerned with predicting future LCC by the feedforward of information about the expected performance which can later be corrected by feedback of information on actual performance. The justification for attempting this monitoring process is that it could result in a substantial saving in costs over the total life of an asset. Any saving of costs must result in increased profits.

The concept of terotechnology embraces this idea of life cycle costing. Terotechnology is defined as 'a combination of management, financial, engineering and other practices applied to physical assets in pursuit of economic life cycle costs'. It is concerned with designing for the reliability and maintainability of physical assets together with the economy of their installation, commissioning, operation and eventual disposal. The physical asset can be a building, an item of plant, a ship, a vehicle, an oil rig or even a whole configuration of plant. The idea of terotechnology may be new but the practices and techniques it embodies are already in use but not necessarily combined together to try to optimize the cost of using physical assets over their whole life. Life cycle costing is really the financial arm of terotechnology.

A typical life cycle will straddle a number of company accounting periods starting with the specification and design of the asset through the sequential stages of its life to its eventual disposal. This life cycle need not be the complete life of the asset if the user plans to dispose of it before it is worn out, or, in the case of a building, alter its use after a certain time. Usually some LCC start with the maker (to be later reimbursed by the purchaser) whilst the remaining LCC commence with the user. The main stages of the LCC of any physical asset can be described as shown in Figure 8.1.

Taking a photocopying machine as an example, the LCC for the user will comprise the original acquisition cost (including specification, design and manufacture of the photocopier) plus the annual operating and maintenance costs

Figure 8.1 Typical life cycle costs

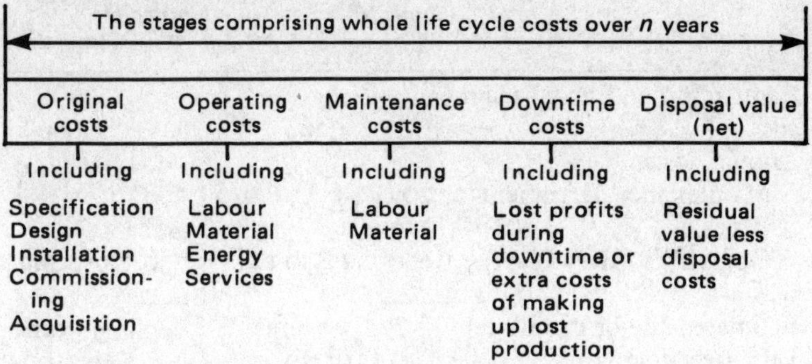

over its total life. These annual costs will include the costs of paper, energy, operator's time and maintenance.

Because these LCC occur in different years we need to bring them to a common point of time by using the new familiar present value concept. When considering actual LCC we must use suitable published indices of labour and material costs to bring them to Year 0 value £s by inflating previous years' figures by the percentage movement in that index.

One very valuable use of this life cycle costing approach is when evaluating alternative machines at the acquisition stage. Very often the advantages of one machine are offset by its disadvantages when compared with an alternative machine of a different design. These advantages and disadvantages will probably not be equal and 'trade-off' studies are required to determine the best buy. In Figure 8.2 (overleaf) the higher initial cost of plain paper Copier A is more than offset by its quicker operating speed, lower maintenance cost and cheaper paper when compared with the less expensive Copier B using specialized paper.

The dearer Copier A is cheaper over its whole life cycle because the extra £1,000 purchase price is more than offset by the savings of £400 p.a. in running costs in each of the next five years. A return of £400 p.a. on an incremental investment of £1,000 is equivalent to a DCF yield of 29%.

Figure 8.2 Five year life cycle costs of two alternative photocopiers

	Copier A £		*Copier B* £	
Acquisition and installation cost		3,000		2,000
Annual costs:				
Maintenance agreement	200		300	
Paper	350		400	
Operator's salary (part)	1,000	1,550 p.a.	1,250	1,950 p.a.
Estimated life of machine		5 years		5 years
LCC over five years		£10,750		£11,750
Present value of LCC assuming a 20% cost of capital		£ 7,636		£ 7,832

This more than satisfies the 20% cost of capital assumed in the above example.

The lowest LCC in present value terms will always denote the most attractive asset from a range of alternatives provided the asset fulfils its purpose adequately. It is important to compare alternatives on a 'like with like' basis. In the case of the photocopiers both alternative machines had the same life expectancy of five years. If this had not been the case the present value LCC for each alternative could be calculated for the number of years which represents the lowest common denominator of all the alternatives' lives. This lowest common denominator may include a number of repetitive life cycles for any one asset.

A more attractive approach to the problem of comparing the LCC of assets with different lives is to express the present value LCC as an annual equivalent sum like a mortgage repayment. In the case of Copier A the LCC of £7,636 is divided by the five year cumulative PV factor at 20% (2.991) to give an annual equivalent cost of £2,553. This annual cost could then be compared with the equivalent annual cost of other copiers expected to last, say, six years and four years respectively.

It is implicit in this example comparing the LCC of alternative copiers that the value (and quality) of the output is the same. If the income generated by alternative assets is not identical then this must be taken into account when comparing their LCC. This could be done by including income and costs in the present value calculations over the whole life of the asset. Alternatively the extra or incremental income of one asset could be netted off against its yearly running costs when comparing the LCC of competing assets.

Every year numerous purchases of buildings and equipment are based on the acquisition cost alone. Purchasing officers and other managers may be beguiled by a seemingly attractive acquisition cost for which 'benefit' their firms will pay in later years through high running costs or a short life. Lowest purchase price does not necessarily minimize total cost over the whole life of the asset and therefore does not maximize profits. If managers have to make decisions on the acquisition of new plant or buildings with sparse information on past or expected performance and costs, then this cannot lead to the best choice. The results may be high operating and maintenance costs, excessive downtime, and wasted effort throughout the organization, which could have been channelled to better use.

This idea of LCC is little more than applied common sense. It is the approach some people take in their personal lives when weighing up the merits of consumer durables like cars. Although we may not carry out precise calculations we are intuitively influenced by differences in expected lives, the cost and frequency of services, fuel consumption and the like. Managers should apply this same approach in their business lives to any proposed purchase of a physical asset be it a building, a machine, a vehicle, an aeroplane or anything else.

All firms in either the public or private sectors can apply LCC to the physical assets they use. These physical assets are alternatively called 'fixed assets' and money spent on acquiring them is called 'capital expenditure'. In central government these physical assets will include, for example, warships and hospitals; in local government LCC can be applied to council houses and leisure pools; in manufacturing industry relevant assets will include the buildings, plant, equipment and vehicles used in the production process; whilst service industries can apply these principles to the buildings, computers and other assets essential to provide a particular service to their clients. LCC can also be applied to consumer durable goods like motor cars and washing machines.

There are two parties interested in the LCC of an asset – the maker and the user. These two parties may occasionally be the same as in the case of a builder constructing an office block for his own use or an engineering firm designing and making a machine for use in their own works. The different approaches of these two parties can perhaps be illustrated by looking at the LCC of a car.

As car owners we have all bemoaned the lack of really adequate anti-corrosion treatment of car bodies at the manufacturing stage. Technological improvements have greatly extended the life of the mechanical parts of a car but thinner panels and salty roads have reduced the average length of life of the car body and hence the life of the car. For relatively little extra cost, some anti-corrosion treatment or the use of alternative metals in the manufacturing process could greatly extend the life of a car. Why then do manufacturers not oblige? They will probably say the customer is looking for the lowest initial cost. Because manufacturers are competing on price in a highly competitive market, one manufacturer will not risk pricing himself out of that market for an intangible benefit the buyer cannot always immediately see.

In this age of high labour and energy costs motorists are coming round to thinking in terms of the LCC of their car rather than just its initial cost or visual appeal. The high costs or petrol and servicing are making buyers more conscious of these subsequent costs so they no longer plump for the lowest initial price of a particular range of cars.

This greater awareness by users is leading manufacturers to examine the design specification of their cars to reduce mud traps, to protect the most vulnerable panels and sections and to design bodies and engines to minimize petrol consumption and reduce service or repair costs. An example of this approach in the late 1970s was by Ford when they introduced their Fiesta model to the market. In this way manufacturers are applying LCC principles to car production by looking at users' future costs and not designing solely to minimize production costs. The resulting design may not be the cheapest car they can produce but the user's total costs over the whole life of the car will be reduced. Users, therefore, should be willing to pay an extra initial cost commensurate with these expected future benefits. It should not be assumed, however, that the application of terotechnology will always lead to a greater initial capital cost.

An industrial application of life cycle costing would be to collate the costs of ownership and use of a physical asset or even a configuration or group of assets. The source of all costing information is the document which originally records the transaction. Typical documents are timecards, stores issue notes and invoices. Accountants use a shorthand system called a 'cost code' to describe the nature of transactions. The cost code is constructed in sections with each section having a specific purpose. For example, blocks of numbers or letters may be used to describe the kind of expense or work carried out, which department did the work, who it was done for and possibly which physical asset was used. Use of cost codes allows a description of the transaction and its value to be fed into computer systems where it is sorted and stored until retrieved later to provide valuable information. An example of this approach is shown below:

Figure 8.3 Typical cost code structure

2 7	5 6 4	8 3 7 2	1 0 6
Originating dept or location number	Number describing the type of expense and the work done	Job, product or project number	Physical asset number

By including a physical asset number in the cost code, all the LCC of acquisition, installation, commissioning, operation, maintenance and disposal can be logged against that particular asset. Although LCC is a relatively simple idea it needs careful thought and planning to realize the potential benefits of its application.

Both manufacturers and users of physical assets can make use of LCC data. Manufacturers should try to get feedback of users' cost data regarding the performance of their equipment. This is the main source of information on the LCC of their products which will encourage them to modify existing models or completely redesign the next generation of equipment or buildings.

Ideally there should be a flow of cost and technical data through the sequential stages of a life cycle. There needs to be a flow of LCC information to allow appraisals to be carried out on modifications, trade-offs and replacement decisions. Costs at one stage of the life cycle are influenced by decisions made at previous stages of the life cycle and hence a feedback of information to those stages is also important. This process may involve both manufacturer and user as the diagram opposite portrays.

The feedback of information from user to manufacturer may not always take place. This may particularly occur when the physical assets concerned are of relatively low value and used singly by many firms. In this situation individual users may not each collect the necessary cost and performance data to feed back to the manufacturer's designers as it would not seem worth the user's costs of collection. Faced with this lack of direct feedback manufacturers can attempt to keep contact with users through their technical representatives. Additionally they can give incentives to users to record data by guaranteeing a certain standard of reliability. They can also offer 'post design' services to rectify faults or modify equipment as necessary. Examples already exist of manufacturers quoting specifications for their equipment in LCC terms.

The other party who can make good use of LCC data on physical assets is the user himself. The following ways

Figure 8.4 Flow of cost and technical information

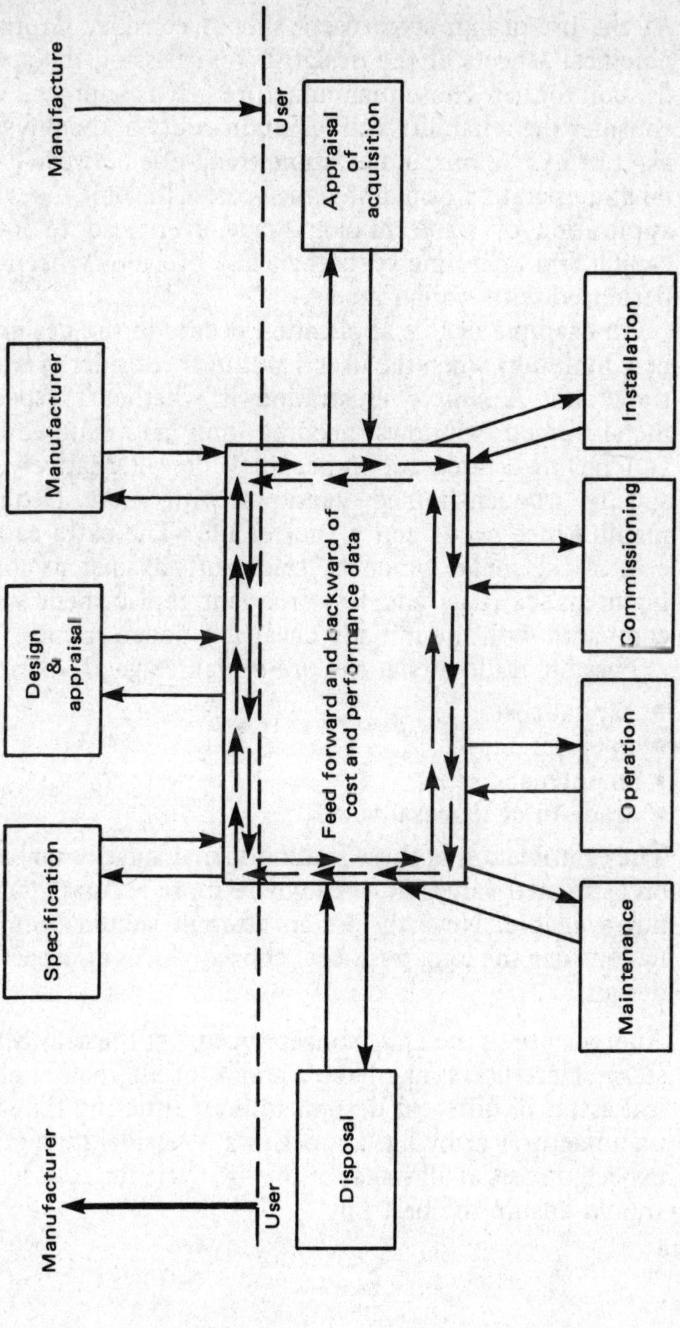

summarize how users can benefit from thinking in life cycle terms.

1 At the pre-design stage users should consider terotechnological aspects of the design before passing the specification to their chosen manufacturer. This approach will consider the reliability and maintainability of the physical asset in LCC terms and examine trade-offs between capital and operating or maintenance costs. In some cases the application of terotechnology may even lead to lower capital and operating costs than had previously been experienced with similar assets.

An example of this application occurs in the design of new buildings when the user's architect considers various trade-offs. A simple illustration is whether to specify metal-framed windows needing minimal maintenance and having a long life expectancy or, alternatively, to specify wooden-framed windows with more frequent maintenance needs and a shorter life. The extra capital cost of the metal windows 'trades-off' against its lower maintenance costs and less frequent replacement when compared with the initially cheaper wooden frames.

Possible trade-offs at the pre-design stage are between:

- capital cost
- operating cost
- maintenance cost
- trade-in or disposal value.

The examination of these trade-offs may have to be based on estimated values in cases where more accurate data is not available. Nevertheless an attempt should be made to consider the long term cost consequences of aspects of design.

2 Another use of the LCC concept occurs at the acquisition stage. Here users may have a choice of alternative physical assets of different designs offered either by the same manufacturer or by his competitors. Consideration of the expected costs at all stages of the life cycle for each model should ensure the best buy.

An example of this approach was discussed earlier when the LCC of two photocopiers were compared. In that case the initially dearer Copier A turned out to be the better buy when compared on a LCC basis with the alternative Copier B. This was because the extra initial cost of Copier A was more than offset by the benefit of lower operating and maintenance costs over its whole life.

3 The monitoring of actual LCC against the budgeted or predicted LCC may highlight the desirability of modifications in service. This does not mean that users have to wait until the end of the asset's life to make such comparisons. If budgeted LCC are broken down into shorter periods, or cost horizons, then more frequent comparisons of budgeted with actual LCC can be made. An example of this approach is contained in Case Study No. 6 in the last chapter. This describes a brewery bottling plant where it was found that much higher losses of beer occurred than had been allowed for in the life cycle budget. Engineering studies to trace the malfunction led to a modification by the brewery. Information fed back to the manufacturer also led to a re-design of this machine for the benefit of subsequent users.

It is possible and beneficial to break into the life cycle at any stage even if a life cycle budget was not prepared before acquisition. For example it may be possible to design out existing high maintenance costs or costs of downtime.

4 Where a user owns a number of similar physical assets and records their LCC he has a valuable source of information to help him decide when to replace such assets. The greater the sample of physical assets then the more representative and statistically reliable the life cycle costs will be. In effect this is another trade-off situation where the higher costs of using and maintaining a physical asset for a further period of time are offset by delaying the cost of a replacement.

An example of this approach is contained in Case Study No. 7 in the last chapter. For the moment let us assume we have been able to calculate the LCC of a physical asset for the same period of years, first assuming the machine is replaced every year, then every two years, every three years and every four years respectively. The present values of these LCC are £75,000, £68,000, £64,000 and £69,000.

If we plot the LCC against the replacement interval on a graph the following picture emerges:

Figure 8.5 Comparison of LCC at different replacement intervals

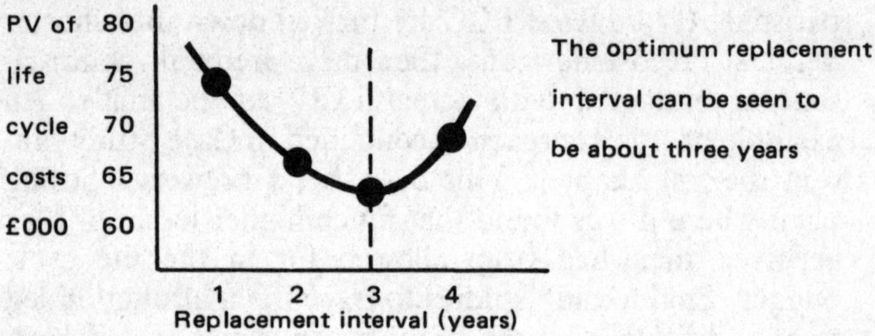

Conclusions

This chapter aims to encourage both manufacturers and users of physical assets to think in life cycle cost terms. Increasing competition in world markets should encourage manufacturers to consider all aspects of the assets they create. The concepts of terotechnology and life cycle costing have an important contribution to make in achieving cost effective designs.

Users should be aware that LCC may be many times more than the original capital cost. Unless attention is paid to subsequent stages of the life cycle a cheap acquisition may prove to be very expensive. Firms should choose physical assets on the basis of predicted LCC and monitor actual LCC to highlight necessary design modifications.

9 Conclusions

Previous chapters have outlined the techniques available to managers when making the important decisions of whether, when and where to invest scarce capital. The superiority of discounting techniques over non-discounting techniques has been demonstrated by the need to take the time value of money into account. Also vitally important is a consideration of taxation, inflation and risk and how these aspects impinge on the profitability of investment. The prime advantage of the discounted cash flow appraisal method is that it is capable of manipulation to allow for these aspects. The benefits of using computers to perform these financial modelling tasks on significant project appraisals cannot be overstressed.

In the final analysis, though, it is people who take decisions not techniques. All the approaches discussed in this introductory book are only aids to decision making to help you make better or more rational decisions but still allowing you to use initiative or a feel for the market by quantifying the likelihood of success. Mathematical models of expected events do not necessarily give concrete answers. Their usefulness lies more in giving weight to a desired course of action or giving an alternative view of a complex problem.

Post audits

Firms should make known that it is company policy to carry out a post audit on investment projects. This means that when the investment proceeds through its various stages of commissioning and operation the actual cash flows should be compared with the expected events. This checking will include capital and operating costs, sales price and volume, commissioning periods and other items. Special attention should be paid to cash flow items found to be significant in sensitivity tests. The actual return earned can also be compared with the predicted DCF yield. To omit this post audit activity means that valuable information is not being fed back to the manager concerned to allow him to gain the experience necessary to improve his future forecasts. Human nature being what it is, the lack of a backward glance will inevitably lead to managers 'estimating' cash flows sufficient to justify acceptance of their pet projects.

There is a case to be made for allocating capital to people rather than to projects. One manager may have a good name for proposing investment initiatives which, on balance, prove to be as profitable as his estimates predicted. Surely he is a more worthy recipient of the firm's scarce funds as opposed to another manager who consistently overestimates the profitability of his schemes?

Criticisms of the DCF yield method

It is hoped by this stage that the basic technique of DCF is not regarded as complicated. Calculations of present value are easy to do with hand-held calculators. The real difficulty lies in preparing the estimated yearly cash flows but this applies to all methods of appraisal including the most rudimentary ones.

More tedious calculations are involved when taking account of inflation and other risks. These have been explained at some length to communicate the purpose and mechanics of such an exercise, not to suggest that an individual manager will perform all the calculations manually. In the first place sophisticated risk treatment is often reserved for projects using a significant amount of capital which eliminates many smaller projects. Secondly, it has been mentioned that computer manufacturers have standard programmes which should fit a firm's requirements when evaluating risk and which can be run by the company accountant if necessary. The purpose of this book is to acquaint managers with techniques that allow them to consider all relevant aspects of an investment. This puts you on an equal footing with the financial specialist but also will help you to identify profitable opportunities without which a firm stagnates.

Another criticism sometimes levied at the DCF yield method is that it occasionally throws up more than one solution rate of interest for the same project. Which one do we take as being correct? The problem only arises where there are negative cash flows in later years after positive cash flows have already been achieved on the investment. It is possible to have as many DCF yields as there are changes in sign in the cash flows. For example, a 'normal' investment has one change from negative cash outlay on the investment to positive cash flows earned on that investment in subsequent years. Provided the cash inflows exceed the cash outflows in total before discounting there can only be one positive DCF yield as there is only one change of sign from negative to positive. However, if a replacement investment is required during the project life, which exceeds the cash inflow in the same year, there will be three changes of sign and possibly three DCF yields.

The easiest way around the problem is to discount any negative cash flow arising during or at the end of a project's life back to the previous year when it is covered by positive cash flows. This discounting is done at the required rate of return using the present value factor for Year 1 to bring it back to its previous year's equivalent value. The DCF yield is then calculated in the normal way now being called the 'extended' DCF yield. It should be appreciated that the negative cash flows arising from tax payments in the last year are not usually significant in this context but can be discounted back to the previous year as described above.

Conflict with the profit and loss account

When firms invest in substantial projects taking two or three years to construct and commission, the effect on the profit and loss account is quite marked. Interest on any borrowed capital invested in the new project will appear as an expense and reduce profits. Alternatively, if new share capital has been raised for the specific project, pre-existing profits are apportioned over the now larger number of shares resulting in a worse performance. When the new project starts to yield profits this situation alters dramatically. Up to the commissioning stage however the profit and loss account will appear at variance with the DCF yield no matter how profitable the investment is expected to be over its whole life. The directors of companies facing this situation may sometimes reject large projects on the grounds that it will adversely affect published profits for a year or two. In no way is this a criticism of the appraisal method but only a truism that the short term view of one year does not necessarily equate with profitability measured over the project's total life. This can be overcome by careful preparation of the shareholders to the short and long term effects.

The nature of investment decisions inevitably means the prediction of future events and therefore luck may play a part in the actual outcome. Good investments depend on the generation of ideas, the use of suitable techniques and management control of the project at all stages. Good luck!

10 Some case studies

Case No. 1 A lease or buy appraisal illustrating aspects of taxation and the timing of lease payments

Carfax Limited have decided to computerize their stores issues to facilitate stocktaking and reordering. This decision was made after a thorough investigation into alternative systems and the likely benefits to be obtained. Management have gone firm on a particular supplier's equipment and related software. They now face the further decision whether to purchase outright or to take up the offer of leasing terms on a fixed price contract for the next five years.

If they buy outright, the total installation will cost £200,000 payable as soon as the system is working to their satisfaction. After one year's free maintenance Carfax will take out a service contract to commence at the start of Year 2. The current cost of this maintenance is £2,000 payable at the beginning of each year, but it will increase in line with inflation estimated at 10% per annum. There is not expected to be any residual value of the equipment at the end of its useful life of five years.

Alternatively, Carfax can lease the installation at an annual rent of £72,000 inclusive of maintenance. These payments apply for the first five years, after which time the lease can be extended if the installation remains in use. The yearly payments for this later period reduce to 5% of the initial cost of the installation.

Carfax require a minimum nominal return of 20% after tax even though their nominal cost of capital is less. The reasoning applied by management is that if they purchase outright they will not be able to invest in other projects yielding a 20% return or more. We can compare the two alternative methods of financing by calculating the NPV cost of each. Initially these calculations are performed using the normal year-end discounting convention as follows:

Net present value cost of the purchase alternative

Year	*Purchase cost* £	*Service contract* £	*52% tax saved* £	*Net cash flow* £	*PV factors @ 20%*	*PV* £
0	− 200,000			− 200,000	1.000	− 200,000
1		− 2,200		− 2,200	.833	− 1,833
2		− 2,420	+ 104,000 + 1,144	+ 102,724	.694	+ 71,290
3		− 2,662	+ 1,258	− 1,404	.579	− 813
4		− 2,928	+ 1,384	− 1,544	.482	− 744
5		—	+ 1,523	+ 1,523	.402	+ 612
					NPV	− £131,488

Net present value cost of the leasing alternative

Year	*Lease payments* £	*52% tax saved* £	*Net cash flow* £	*PV factors @ 20%*	*PV* £
0			–		
1	− 72,000		− 72,000	.833	− 59,976
2	− 72,000	+ 37,440	− 34,560		
3	− 72,000	+ 37,440	− 34,560		
4	− 72,000	+ 37,440	− 34,560	2.158 (years 2–5)	− 74,580
5	− 72,000	+ 37,440	− 34,560		
6		+ 37,440	+ 37,440	.335	+ 12,542
				NPV	− £122,014

Notes on calculations

1 The service contract is payable at the end of Year 1 in respect of Year 2 therefore the £2,200 represents the original £2,000 enhanced by 10% inflation. Later years are similarly increased by 10% p.a. with the last payment occurring at the end of Year 4 in respect of Year 5.

2 Payments for the service contract will be an allowable expense for tax purposes as they reduce otherwise taxable

profits. Owing to the time lag in making corporation tax payments, the amount of tax saved will accordingly be lagged one year.

3 It is assumed that profits exist in Carfax sufficient to claim a 100% capital allowance immediately on the whole cost of the installation. This has the effect of saving tax on £200,000 of profits, yielding a benefit of £104,000. If the purchase takes place early in the accounting year the reduced tax payments will be lagged two years. This assumption has been made here so as not to make the purchase alternative look more attractive than may be the case. If Carfax had no immediate profits to offset this capital allowance against, this would greatly reduce the benefit of the tax saving and make the purchase alternative less attractive.

4 Lease payments are also an allowable expense against tax so these savings are subject to the same time lag as in note 2.

5 If the useful life of the installation does not reach five years Carfax is tied to the financial agreements expressed in the NPV calculations above and the choice is not affected. If the life exceeds five years the service payments will continue on the purchase alternative or the leasing payments reduce to £10,000 p.a. less tax relief. Such longer life makes leasing less attractive although the PV factors are relatively small at Year 6 and beyond.

6 On a strict interpretation of the NPV cost of each alternative it may appear £9,000 cheaper to lease rather than to buy the installation. Two more questions of timing must be mentioned before jumping to such a conclusion.

(i) On the purchase alternative a two year lag was assumed for the tax saved by the capital allowance. Tax payments can only be specifically identified for any one company when the exact purchase date is related to the company accounting year and both the size and date of dividend payments are known. These matters are discussed in Chapter 4. Suffice it to say that if only a one year lag applies to the tax saved by the allowance it reduces the NPV cost by as much as £14,500. This has the effect of reversing the initial choice of leasing as the cheaper alternative.

(ii) It has been assumed in the calculations that all financial transactions take place at year-ends. This is probably valid for all transactions bar the lease payments of £72,000. If these payments occur throughout the year their present value cost will be increased in Years 1–5 as money is paid out sooner than it would be at year-ends. The following figures summarize the difference:

PV cost of 5 payments of £72,000 at year-ends	£215,352
PV cost of 5 payments of £72,000 during each year	£227,520
Difference*	£12,168

Conclusions

Taking all factors into consideration purchasing may be considered more attractive to Carfax than leasing the installation. This is based on the assumptions that leasing payments will most likely occur during each year; that the life may exceed five years; and that tax relief on the purchase may not be as late as the case assumed.

Case No. 2 Example of a replacement decision where alternative courses of action have different lives

The Seaton Engineering Co. are considering whether to replace or repair a particular machine which has just broken

* The difference between the two conventions is most marked in the combination of either a low discount rate with a long life or a high discount rate with a short life.

down. Last year this machine cost £20,000 to run and maintain. These costs have been increasing in real terms in recent years with the age of the machine. A further useful life of five years is expected if immediate repairs costing £19,000 are carried out. If the machine is not repaired it will be sold immediately to realize about £5,000.

Alternatively, the company can buy a new machine for £49,000 with an expected life of ten years. In this case running and maintenance costs will reduce to £14,000 each year and are not expected to increase much in real terms for a few years at least. Seaton Engineering regard a nominal return of 20% as a minimum requirement on any new investment.

A difficulty which arises in this situation is the difference in life expectancy between the two alternatives. Clearly we cannot use the total NPV cost over five years to compare with a NPV cost over ten years. If we assume replacement will take place after five years if we repair the existing machine then we are faced with a fifteen year total which again is not comparable with ten years.

One way to tackle this problem of unequal lives is to compare alternatives on an annual cost basis. This technique was first mentioned in Chapter 8 and basically consists of reducing the capital cost to an annual basis. We do this by calculating what is equivalent to the yearly repayment on a building society mortgage. The amount needed each year to repay £1 is the reciprocal of the cumulative present value factor for that year. For example, if we refer back to Figure 2.4 in Chapter 2 the annual repayment for each of ten years on a £20,000 mortgage at 12% is found from the calculation £20,000 $\times \frac{1}{5.650} =$ £3,540.

We can now apply this technique to the replacement decision facing Seaton Engineering by comparing both alternatives on an annual cost basis which will take into account the different life expectancies as overleaf.

The difference of £2,335 in the annual costs represents the saving achieved from buying the new replacement machine rather than repairing the old. This difference will widen if the real cost of operating the old machine increases

Repair existing machine	
Resale value if sold now	£5,000
Cost of repairs now	£19,000
Total cost at Year 0	£24,000
Annual equivalent cost (for five years)	£8,024*
Running and maintenance cost p.a.	£20,000
Total annual cost	£28,024

Buy replacement machine	
Purchase cost of new machine	£49,000
Annual equivalent cost (for ten years)	£11,689†
Running and maintenance costs p.a.	£14,000
Total annual cost	£25,689

Notes: Tax has been ignored for simplicity but must be allowed for in reality.

* The annual equivalent cost has been calculated from $\frac{£24{,}000}{2{,}991}$

† The annual equivalent cost has been calculated from $\frac{£49{,}000}{4{,}192}$

An alternative treatment of the £5,000 resale value of the existing machine is to omit it from the first calculation and deduct £5,000 from the cost of the new machine to give a net purchase cost of £44,000.

with age whilst the operating cost of the new machine does not change much for the next few years. Inflation will also widen the gap between the two alternatives having more effect on the higher running costs on the existing machine so making the new machine even more attractive.

Tax relief will apply to all the costs in both alternatives. A capital allowance will be claimed on the new machine whereas repair and running costs will automatically get relief through their inclusion in the profit and loss account. Assuming Seaton Engineering are able to claim the 100% capital allowance immediately this will be of more benefit than the relief obtained on the repair cost and higher running costs of the existing machine. This adds to the attractions of buying the new machine.

Case No. 3 Illustration of an expansion/diversification project incorporating aspects of taxation and inflation

Progressive Limited require a nominal return of 20% after tax on any new investment. Management are considering a proposal to make and sell a new product by installing new plant in existing premises. No alternative use is envisaged for this space in the foreseeable future. The initial investment totals £180,000 comprising £100,000 of new plant and £80,000 working capital of which one half represents stocks of materials and finished goods. A product life of five years is anticipated after which time the plant will have remaining value of about £10,000 at today's prices, and the working capital will be recovered. Situated in a Special Development Area, Progressive Limited fully expect to receive a grant of 22% of the cost of the new plant in about one year's time.

Sales are budgeted at £200,000 for each of the next five years and operating costs (excluding depreciation) are put at £150,000. Inflation will affect both of these figures which are expressed at today's prices. The rate of inflation is expected to be about 10% p.a. and will also affect working capital requirements and the resale value of the plant. This estimate of inflation is not regarded as too critical as increased costs can be quickly recovered with little effect on sales volume.

Corporation tax is currently 52% but sufficient profits are being made elsewhere in the business to claim the 100% capital allowance. A two year lag is assumed by Progressive Limited for such tax savings. Stock relief will apply to the original and additional money value of stock each year. It is not thought that the special price index for Progressive's stocks will differ significantly from the general rate of inflation.

The various constituent items of the net cash flow can be set out in separate columns for simplicity and a present value calculation conducted at the minimum required rate of 20% as shown on the next page:

Progressive Limited – Calculation of the NPV @ 20% on an expansion project assuming 10% inflation applies to all relevant cash flows

	(1)	(2)	(3)	(4)	(5)	(6)	(7)	(8)	(9)	(10)	(11)	(12)
Year	*Investment in plant*	*Capital allowance*	*Tax saved on allowance*	*Investment in working capital*	*52% tax saved on stock relief*	*Sales*	*Costs*	*Taxable profits*	*52% tax on profits*	*Net cash flow*	*PV factors @ 20%*	*PV*
	£		£	£	£	£	£	£	£	£		£
0	– 100,000	100,000		– 80,000						– 180,000	1.000	– 180,000
	Grant											
1	+ 22,000			– 8,000		+ 220,000	– 165,000	+ 55,000		+ 69,000	.833	+ 57,477
2			+ 52,000	– 8,800	+ 20,800	+ 242,000	– 181,500	+ 60,500	– 28,600	+ 95,900	.694	+ 66,555
3				– 9,680	+ 2,080	+ 266,200	– 199,650	+ 66,550	– 31,460	+ 27,490	.579	+ 15,917
4				– 10,648	+ 2,288	+ 292,820	– 219,615	+ 73,205	– 34,606	+ 30,239	.482	+ 14,575
	Resale											
5	+ 16,105	(16,105)		+ 117,128	+ 2,517	+ 322,102	– 241,577	+ 80,525	– 38,067	+ 178,208	.402	+ 71,640
6			– 8,375		+ 2,768				– 41,873	– 47,480	.335	– 15,906
											NPV	+ £30,258

Conclusion: The project is viable as it meets the requirement of a nominal return of 20% after tax. (Note: Clawback of stock relief can occur in certain exceptional circumstances.)

The surplus NPV of £30,258 indicates that a considerably higher rate of interest could have been deducted. Progressive can discover this solution rate (i.e. DCF yield) by trial and error. Supposing a 30% rate of interest was chosen the NPV calculation is as follows:

	Net cash flow £	*PV factors @ 30%*	*PV* £
Year 0	− 180,000	1.000	− 180,000
1	+ 69,000	.769	+ 53,061
2	+ 95,900	.592	+ 56,773
3	+ 27,490	.455	+ 12,508
4	+ 30,239	.350	+ 10,584
5	+ 178,208	.269	+ 47,938
6	− 47,480	.207	− 9,828
		NPV	− £8,964

By interpolation with the previous NPV surplus of £30,258 at 20% it appears that every 1% change in the discount rate alters the NPV by about £3,900. To eliminate the above deficit of nearly £9,000 will require a reduction in the 30% interest rate of about 2%. The DCF yield can therefore be interpolated at about 28% which we would go on to calculate in practice.

After allowing for inflation at 10% on the relevant cash flows and incorporating all tax transactions in the year they occur we can assume Progressive's management will accept this project as quite viable. The expected DCF yield of 28% comfortably exceeds the 20% minimum required. Further tests on the sensitivity of the return to variations in the cash flows can be carried out or probabilities applied to different sets of cash flows. These matters are discussed in previous chapters and applied in a later case study.

Case No. 4 Illustration of the use of probability theory in dealing with uncertain future costs and revenues

The management of Shop Developers Limited are considering the feasibility of a new development to build and let shops on the outskirts of a large town. Depending on the exact design of the buildings the capital cost will be between £2 m and £2.2 m with greater emphasis on the lower figure. More doubt exists as to the level of net rental income. It could be as low as £200,000 but with an attractive layout and a little luck it could be as much as £260,000 each year. The realistic life of the development is put at 25 years.

Shop Developers require a return on investment of 9%. This may seem low but it should be borne in mind that much of the capital is borrowed at a fixed rate of interest which does not increase when rents are periodically reviewed. Such future increases in rent will compensate for inflation as well as reflect the demand for such properties.

To facilitate the decision whether to proceed with the development or not, the project team have been asked to assess the likelihood of the eventual outcomes. More specifically, they have been asked to assign probability factors to both the capital cost and the net income from rent. More than one value can be assumed for each of these variable items to cover the range of possibilities. The values chosen by the project team with their respective probability factors are shown below:

Capital cost	*Probability*	*Annual rent*	*Probability*
£2.0 m	0.7	£200,000	0.1
£2.2 m	0.3	£220,000	0.3
	1.0	£240,000	0.4
		£260,000	0.2
			1.0

Instead of calculating the DCF yield from just one estimate

of rent and one capital cost it is possible to combine the likelihood of all the possible values in the computation. For example the weighted average capital cost can be expressed as:

£2.0 m × 0.7	= £1.40 m
£2.2 m × 0.3	= £0.66 m
Weighted average cost	= £2.06 m

Similarly the four possible rent values can be used together with their respective probabilities to find the weighted average annual rent:

£200,000 × 0.1	= £20,000
£220,000 × 0.3	= £66,000
£240,000 × 0.4	= £96,000
£260,000 × 0.2	= £52,000
Weighted average rent	= £234,000 p.a.

The expected DCF yield can now be interpolated from the cumulative PV table for 25 years. The relevant factor is found from the calculation in £2.06 m/£234,000 = 8.8 which equates to the 10% rate of interest. The initial return on the investment is therefore expected to be 10% which is the weighted average of all the possibilities considered.

The next question posed by the management of Shop Developers concerns the level of confidence that the project team have in the development yielding a satisfactory return of 9% or more. There are eight possible combined events from the pairing of one of two capital costs with one of four annual rents. For each of these combined events we need to calculate the DCF yield and the probability of the two values combining together. The DCF yields are calculated from the cumulative PV table and the combined probability from the multiplication of the two relevant probabilities as shown overleaf.

There is only one combined event which does not yield a satisfactory return. This occurs when the lowest rent envisaged combines with the highest capital cost to give a

	Capital cost			
	£2.0 m (0.7)		£2.2 m (0.3)	
Annual rent	*DCF yield*	*Combined probability*	*DCF yield*	*Combined probability*
£200,000 (.1)	9%	(.07)	8%	(.03)
£220,000 (.3)	10%	(.21)	9%	(.09)
£240,000 (.4)	11%	(.28)	10%	(.12)
£260,000 (.2)	12%	(.14)	11%	(.06)

DCF yield of 8%. The chance of this combination occurring is .03 or 3%, whilst the chance of the rate of return being 9% or more is 97%. We can use this 97% as the level of confidence Shop Developers have in a satisfactory outcome to the development. Because the expected DCF yield of 10% is slightly higher than the minimum required and the level of confidence in a satisfactory outcome exceptionally high at 97% we can assume this project will proceed.

Case No. 5 Illustration of inflation being incorporated in the cash flows and its effect on a large terminal value

Gosforth Brewery Limited are considering refurbishing one of their managed houses at a cost of £50,000. The property is currently worth £200,000 and the refurbishing is expected to last five years by which time it is assumed the property will be worth £450,000.

The increase in trade resulting from refurbishing is valued at £12,000 for the first year and is expected to rise in line with inflation over the next four years at 10% p.a.

The directors normally require a nominal return of at least 15% and the appraisal opposite (above) was put forward for their approval.

Just as they were about to approve this project on the grounds that it seemed to satisfy the minimum target rate of return of 15%, one director queried this analysis. 'If the

	Net cash flow £	*PV factors @ 15%*	*PV* £
Year 0	− 200,000 − 50,000	1.000	− 250,000
1	+ 12,000	.870	+ 10,440
2	+ 13,200	.756	+ 9,979
3	+ 14,520	.658	+ 9,554
4	+ 15,972	.572	+ 9,136
5	+ 17,569 + 450,000	.497	+ 232,382
		NPV	+ £21,491

(Note: Taxation is ignored in this example for clarity.)

property is going to rise in value whether we refurbish or not,' he said, 'should we not justify the £50,000 investment in refurbishing by the increased profits from trade alone, excluding the rise in property value?'

After some heated discussion it was agreed to look at the project again and the accountant was requested to do some quick sums.

His revised appraisal now appeared to show that the increased trade did not justify the refurbishing cost:

	Net cash flow £	*PV factors @ 15%*	*PV* £
Year 0	− 50,000	1.000	− 50,000
1	+ 12,000	.870	+ 10,440
2	+ 13,200	.756	+ 9,979
3	+ 14,520	.658	+ 9,554
4	+ 15,972	.572	+ 9,136
5	+ 17,569	.497	+ 8,732
		NPV	− £2,159

The directors were unwilling to approve the scheme and asked the marketing director to consider ways of increasing trade to make the scheme viable. The amount of extra trade required can be calculated by a further trial and interpolation of the results. Assuming £13,000 was chosen as the first year value the NPV calculation results in a surplus as follows:

	Net cash flow £	*PV factors @ 15%*	*PV* £
Year 0	− 50,000	1.000	− 50,000
1	+ 13,000	.870	+ 11,310
2	+ 14,300	.756	+ 10,811
3	+ 15,730	.658	+ 10,350
4	+ 17,303	.572	+ 9,897
5	+ 19,033	.497	+ 9,459
		NPV	+ £1,827

By interpolation the increase in initial trade required to give a 15% return on the refurbishing cost is about £12,500 as the NPVs of − £2,159 and + £1,827 are almost equidistant to the zero NPV required for a 15% return.

Case No. 6 Illustration of life cycle costing applied to a physical asset already in use

Durham Brewery have a steady market for one of their bottled beers and have recently installed a new bottle-washing and -filling machine of a different type to that previously used. The project team were keen to know how the machine performed against the manufacturer's specification and their own estimates. With this in mind they prepared a life cycle cost budget for the new machine and decided to monitor the actual costs in use. A summary of the LCC budget is shown opposite together with the actual costs for the first year of operation.

In general terms the machine performed very much as expected except in one important area. A certain amount of bottle breakage and associated beer losses are inevitable and a reasonable allowance was made by the project team

Life cycle cost of bottle-washing and -filling machine

Annual costs

	Budget £	Budget %	Actual £	
Capital	22,000	16.6	22,000	Annual equivalent cost of purchase and installation
Operation	9,800	7.4	10,150	Labour
	39,000	29.5	37,820	Steam
	15,000	11.3	15,700	Electricity
	9,000	6.8	8,750	Water
Maintenance	8,700	6.6	12,500	Labour
	3,200	2.4	7,590	Materials and parts
	500	0.4	500	Holding costs of parts
Bottling losses	25,000	18.9	47,350	Glass breakage and beer spillage
	£132.200	100%	£162,360	

(Note: The total beer cost is not included as a cost of the machine.)

in the light of experience. The actual cost of the breakages and spoilt beer was nearly twice the amount predicted in the budget. Compared to the capital cost for the year these bottling losses were twice the cost of the machine itself. It was apparent that substantial savings would result from the elimination of the source of the malfunction. Engineering studies were carried out and modifications to the machine were implemented. The manufacturer was also involved even though the brewery carried out their own modification. Without feedback from such users, manufacturers are not able to 'design-out' faults and imperfections. Only £20,000 was spent on the modification and this was repaid by the savings achieved in the first year.

Case No. 7 Illustration of life cycle cost data used to formulate a replacement policy

Buzby National Telephone Service use a substantial fleet of vans of varying ages up to four years old. Each van has an individual asset number against which all fuel, oil, maintenance and repair costs are charged. Using this data it has been possible to extract the trends of the costs relative to the age of the vehicle. These costs were then converted to today's prices by use of appropriate price indices. The following information relating to the present type of vehicle is all expressed in current purchasing power £s:

1 Purchase cost of new van £6,000

2 Trade-in value when: One year old £4,000
Two years old £2,500
Three years old £1,300
Four years old £500

3 Fuel consumption increases with the age of the vehicle partly through wear but also because the design improvements of more recent models result in fuel economies. Maintenance, repair and parts replacement also increase in cost as the vehicle ages, particularly after two years. These costs (at today's prices) are as follows:

	Fuel cost p.a.	*Maintenance and repair cost p.a.*
0–1 Years	£2,500	£200
1–2 Years	£2,600	£350
2–3 Years	£2,820	£700
3–4 Years	£3,200	£1,750

The nominal cost of borrowing from the government is about 15.5%. A nominal rate is used to discount cash flows expressed in future value £s. The above costs are all expressed at today's prices and are not inflated year by year for inflation expected to fluctuate around 10% p.a. There are therefore two alternative procedures we can follow. We can either inflate all costs and values by 10% p.a. and discount the LCC at 15.5%, or we can leave the money values in today's £s and discount the LCC at 5%. (With inflation at 10% p.a. a nominal return of 15.5% equates to a real return of 5%.) For simplicity of explanation of the yearly cash flows the latter course of action is adopted here and a 5% discount rate is used in the present value calculation.

If vehicles can be kept up to four years it is essential to examine the possibility of replacing them up to this age. Therefore Buzby is faced with four alternative replacement intervals – when the vans are one year, two years, three years and four years old respectively. The lowest common multiple of these four replacement intervals is twelve years for which period we shall compute the net present value of the life cycle costs as follows:

LCC of a service van assuming replacement each year for a total period of twelve years

(1)	(2)	(3)	(4)	(5)	(6)	(7)	(8)
Year	*Purchase cost*	*Trade-in value*	*Fuel cost*	*Maintenance & repair cost*	*Net cash flow*	*PV factors @ 5%*	*PV*
	£	£	£	£	£		£
0	− 6,000				− 6,000	1.000	− 6,000
1	− 6,000	+ 4,000	− 2,500	− 200	− 4,700		
2	− 6,000	+ 4,000	− 2,500	− 200	− 4,700		
3	− 6,000	+ 4,000	− 2,500	− 200	− 4,700		
4	− 6,000	+ 4,000	− 2,500	− 200	− 4,700		
5	− 6,000	+ 4,000	− 2,500	− 200	− 4,700		
6	− 6,000	+ 4,000	− 2,500	− 200	− 4,700		
7	− 6,000	+ 4,000	− 2,500	− 200	− 4,700	8.306	− 39,038
8	− 6,000	+ 4,000	− 2,500	− 200	− 4,700		
9	− 6,000	+ 4,000	− 2,500	− 200	− 4,700		
10	− 6,000	+ 4,000	− 2,500	− 200	− 4,700		
11	− 6,000	+ 4,000	− 2,500	− 200	− 4,700		
12	–	+ 4,000	− 2,500	− 200	+ 1,300	.557	+ 724
						NPV	− £44,314

The cost of buying and running one service van and replacing it at the end of each year has a total PV cost of £44,314 over a twelve year period. This can now be compared with the equivalent PV cost on the assumption that the van is replaced every two years instead of each year as follows:

LCC of a service van assuming replacement every two years for a total period of twelve years

(1) Year	(2) Purchase cost £	(3) Trade-in value £	(4) Fuel cost £	(5) Maintenance & repair cost £	(6) Net cash flow £	(7) PV factors @ 5%	(8) PV £
0	− 6,000				− 6,000	1.000	− 6,000
1			− 2,500	− 200	− 2,700	.952	− 2,570
2	− 6,000	+ 2,500	− 2,600	− 350	− 6,450	.907	− 5,850
3			− 2,500	− 200	− 2,700	.864	− 2,333
4	− 6,000	+ 2,500	− 2,600	− 350	− 6,450	.823	− 5,308
5			− 2,500	− 200	− 2,700	.784	− 2,117
6	− 6,000	+ 2,500	− 2,600	− 350	− 6,450	.746	− 4,812
7			− 2,500	− 200	− 2,700	.711	− 1,920
8	− 6,000	+ 2,500	− 2,600	− 350	− 6,450	.677	− 4,367
9			− 2,500	− 200	− 2,700	.645	− 1,742
10	− 6,000	+ 2,500	− 2,600	− 350	− 6,450	.614	− 3,960
11			− 2,500	− 200	− 2,700	.585	− 1,580
12		+ 2,500	− 2,600	− 350	− 450	.557	− 251
						NPV	− £42,810

The cost of buying and running a service van and replacing it every two years can be seen to be less than the NPV cost of £44,314 resulting from replacing each year. We now need to calculate similar NPVs for a three year replacement interval and a four year interval. The reader can attempt these for himself and will find them to be £42,752 and £44,874 respectively. We can summarize the results as follows:

Replacement interval	*NPV cost*
One year	£44,314
Two years	£42,810
Three years	£42,752
Four years	£44,874

From inspection it can be seen that the one year and four year replacement intervals are not the cheapest but that replacing every two or three years would be more economic. There is little to choose between the costs of the middle values and the replacement policy will be determined by non-financial factors like image.

Note: The alternative approach of inflating the yearly cash flows and discounting at the nominal rate of 15.5% will lead to exactly the same result and will have to be adopted when we cannot make the assumption that all costs and trade-in values will inflate at an equal rate. In the private sector we must also incorporate tax transactions in the yearly cash flows.

Appendix A
Present value of £1

n Year	5%	6%	7%	8%	9%	10%	11%	12%	13%
0	1.000	1.000	1.000	1.000	1.000	1.000	1.000	1.000	1.000
1	.952	.943	.935	.926	.917	.909	.901	.893	.885
2	.907	.890	.873	.857	.842	.826	.812	.797	.783
3	.864	.840	.816	.794	.772	.751	.731	.712	.693
4	.823	.792	.763	.735	.708	.683	.659	.636	.613
5	.784	.747	.713	.681	.650	.621	.593	.567	.543
6	.746	.705	.666	.630	.596	.564	.535	.507	.480
7	.711	.665	.623	.583	.547	.513	.482	.452	.425
8	.677	.627	.582	.540	.502	.467	.434	.404	.376
9	.645	.592	.544	.500	.460	.424	.391	.361	.333
10	.614	.558	.508	.463	.422	.386	.352	.322	.295
11	.585	.527	.475	.429	.388	.350	.317	.287	.261
12	.557	.497	.444	.397	.356	.319	.286	.257	.231
13	.530	.469	.415	.368	.326	.290	.258	.229	.204
14	.505	.442	.388	.340	.299	.263	.232	.205	.181
15	.481	.417	.362	.315	.275	.239	.209	.183	.160
16	.458	.394	.339	.292	.252	.218	.188	.163	.141
17	.436	.371	.317	.270	.231	.198	.170	.146	.125
18	.416	.350	.296	.250	.212	.180	.153	.130	.111
19	.396	.331	.277	.232	.194	.164	.138	.116	.098
20	.377	.312	.258	.215	.178	.149	.124	.104	.087
25	.295	.233	.184	.146	.116	.092	.074	.059	.047
30	.231	.174	.131	.099	.075	.057	.044	.033	.026
35	.181	.130	.094	.068	.049	.036	.026	.019	.014
40	.142	.097	.067	.046	.032	.022	.015	.011	.008
45	.111	.073	.048	.031	.021	.014	.009	.006	.004
50	.087	.054	.034	.021	.013	.009	.005	.003	.002

Note: The above present value factors are based on year-end interest calculations.

14%	15%	16%	17%	18%	19%	20%	21%	22%	23%
1.000	1.000	1.000	1.000	1.000	1.000	1.000	1.000	1.000	1.000
.877	.870	.862	.855	.847	.840	.833	.826	.820	.813
.769	.756	.743	.731	.718	.706	.694	.683	.672	.661
.675	.658	.641	.624	.609	.593	.579	.564	.551	.537
.592	.572	.552	.534	.516	.499	.482	.467	.451	.437
.519	.497	.476	.456	.437	.419	.402	.386	.370	.355
.456	.432	.410	.390	.370	.352	.335	.319	.303	.289
.400	.376	.354	.333	.314	.296	.279	.263	.249	.235
.351	.327	.305	.285	.266	.249	.233	.218	.204	.191
.308	.284	.263	.243	.225	.209	.194	.180	.167	.155
.270	.247	.227	.208	.191	.176	.162	.149	.137	.126
.237	.215	.195	.178	.162	.148	.135	.123	.112	.103
.208	.187	.168	.152	.137	.124	.112	.102	.092	.083
.182	.163	.145	.130	.116	.104	.093	.084	.075	.068
.160	.141	.125	.111	.099	.088	.078	.069	.062	.055
.140	.123	.108	.095	.084	.074	.065	.057	.051	.045
.123	.107	.093	.081	.071	.062	.054	.047	.042	.036
.108	.093	.080	.069	.060	.052	.045	.039	.034	.030
.095	.081	.069	.059	.051	.044	.038	.032	.028	.024
.083	.070	.060	.051	.043	.037	.031	.027	.023	.020
.073	.061	.051	.043	.037	.031	.026	.022	.019	.016
.038	.030	.025	.020	.016	.013	.011	.009	.007	.006
.020	.015	.012	.009	.007	.005	.004	.003	.003	.002
.010	.008	.006	.004	.003	.002	.002	.001	.001	.001
.005	.004	.003	.002	.001	.001	.001	.000	.000	.000
.003	.002	.001	.001	.001	.000	.000	.000	.000	.000
.001	.001	.001	.000	.000	.000	.000	.000	.000	.000

Note: The above present value factors are based on year-end interest calculations.

n Year	24%	25%	26%	27%	28%	29%	30%	35%	40%
0	1.000	1.000	1.000	1.000	1.000	1.000	1.000	1.000	1.000
1	.807	.800	.794	.787	.781	.775	.769	.741	.714
2	.650	.640	.630	.620	.610	.601	.592	.549	.510
3	.524	.512	.500	.488	.477	.466	.455	.406	.364
4	.423	.410	.397	.384	.373	.361	.350	.301	.260
5	.341	.328	.315	.303	.291	.280	.269	.223	.186
6	.275	.262	.250	.238	.227	.217	.207	.165	.133
7	.222	.210	.198	.188	.178	.168	.159	.122	.095
8	.179	.168	.157	.148	.139	.130	.123	.091	.068
9	.144	.134	.125	.116	.108	.101	.094	.067	.048
10	.116	.107	.099	.092	.085	.078	.073	.050	.035
11	.094	.086	.079	.072	.066	.061	.056	.037	.025
12	.076	.069	.062	.057	.052	.047	.043	.027	.018
13	.061	.055	.050	.045	.040	.037	.033	.020	.013
14	.049	.044	.039	.035	.032	.028	.025	.015	.009
15	.040	.035	.031	.028	.025	.022	.020	.011	.006
16	.032	.028	.025	.022	.019	.017	.015	.008	.005
17	.026	.023	.020	.017	.015	.013	.012	.006	.003
18	.021	.018	.016	.014	.012	.010	.009	.005	.002
19	.017	.014	.012	.011	.009	.008	.007	.003	.002
20	.014	.012	.010	.008	.007	.006	.005	.002	.001
25	.005	.004	.003	.003	.002	.002	.001	.001	.000
30	.002	.001	.001	.001	.001	.000	.000	.000	.000
35	.001	.000	.000	.000	.000	.000	.000	.000	.000
40	.000	.000	.000	.000	.000	.000	.000	.000	.000
45	.000	.000	.000	.000	.000	.000	.000	.000	.000
50	.000	.000	.000	.000	.000	.000	.000	.000	.000

Note: The above present value factors are based on year-end interest calculations.

Appendix B
Cumulative present value of £1 per annum

n Year	5%	6%	7%	8%	9%	10%	11%	12%	13%
1	.952	.943	.935	.926	.917	.909	.901	.893	.885
2	1.859	1.833	1.808	1.783	1.759	1.736	1.713	1.690	1.668
3	2.723	2.673	2.624	2.577	2.531	2.487	2.444	2.402	2.361
4	3.546	3.465	3.387	3.312	3.240	3.170	3.102	3.037	2.974
5	4.329	4.212	4.100	3.993	3.890	3.791	3.696	3.605	3.517
6	5.076	4.917	4.767	4.623	4.486	4.355	4.231	4.111	3.998
7	5.786	5.582	5.389	5.206	5.033	4.868	4.712	4.564	4.423
8	6.463	6.210	5.971	5.747	5.535	5.335	5.146	4.968	4.799
9	7.108	6.802	6.515	6.247	5.995	5.759	5.537	5.328	5.132
10	7.722	7.360	7.024	6.710	6.418	6.145	5.889	5.650	5.426
11	8.306	7.887	7.499	7.139	6.805	6.495	6.207	5.938	5.687
12	8.863	8.384	7.943	7.536	7.161	6.814	6.492	6.194	5.918
13	9.394	8.853	8.358	7.904	7.487	7.103	6.750	6.424	6.122
14	9.899	9.295	8.745	8.244	7.786	7.367	6.982	6.628	6.302
15	10.380	9.712	9.108	8.559	8.061	7.606	7.191	6.811	6.462
16	10.838	10.106	9.447	8.851	8.313	7.824	7.379	6.974	6.604
17	11.274	10.477	9.763	9.122	8.544	8.022	7.549	7.120	6.729
18	11.690	10.828	10.059	9.372	8.756	8.201	7.702	7.250	6.840
19	12.085	11.158	10.336	9.604	8.950	8.365	7.839	7.366	6.938
20	12.462	11.470	10.594	9.818	9.129	8.514	7.963	7.469	7.025
25	14.094	12.783	11.654	10.675	9.823	9.077	8.422	7.843	7.330
30	15.372	13.765	12.409	11.258	10.274	9.427	8.694	8.055	7.496
35	16.374	14.498	12.948	11.655	10.567	9.644	8.855	8.176	7.586
40	17.159	15.046	13.332	11.925	10.757	9.779	8.951	8.244	7.634
45	17.774	15.456	13.606	12.108	10.881	9.863	9.008	8.283	7.661
50	18.256	15.762	13.801	12.234	10.962	9.915	9.042	8.305	7.675

Note: The above present value factors are based on year-end interest calculations.

n Year	14%	15%	16%	17%	18%	19%	20%	21%	22%	23%
1	.877	.870	.862	.855	.847	.840	.833	.826	.820	.813
2	1.647	1.626	1.605	1.585	1.566	1.546	1.528	1.510	1.492	1.474
3	2.322	2.283	2.246	2.210	2.174	2.140	2.106	2.074	2.042	2.011
4	2.914	2.855	2.798	2.743	2.690	2.639	2.589	2.540	2.494	2.448
5	3.433	3.352	3.274	3.199	3.127	3.058	2.991	2.926	2.864	2.804
6	3.889	3.784	3.685	3.589	3.498	3.410	3.326	3.245	3.167	3.092
7	4.288	4.160	4.039	3.922	3.812	3.706	3.605	3.508	3.416	3.327
8	4.639	4.487	4.344	4.207	4.078	3.954	3.837	3.726	3.619	3.518
9	4.946	4.772	4.607	4.451	4.303	4.163	4.031	3.905	3.786	3.673
10	5.216	5.019	4.833	4.659	4.494	4.339	4.192	4.054	3.923	3.799
11	5.453	5.234	5.029	4.836	4.656	4.486	4.327	4.177	4.035	3.902
12	5.660	5.421	5.197	4.988	4.793	4.610	4.439	4.278	4.127	3.985
13	5.842	5.583	5.342	5.118	4.910	4.715	4.533	4.362	4.203	4.053
14	6.002	5.724	5.468	5.229	5.008	4.802	4.611	4.432	4.265	4.108
15	6.142	5.847	5.575	5.324	5.092	4.876	4.675	4.490	4.315	4.153
16	6.265	5.954	5.669	5.405	5.162	4.938	4.730	4.536	4.357	4.190
17	6.373	6.047	5.749	5.475	5.222	4.990	4.775	4.576	4.391	4.219
18	6.467	6.128	5.818	5.534	5.273	5.033	4.812	4.608	4.419	4.243
19	6.550	6.198	5.877	5.584	5.316	5.070	4.844	4.635	4.442	4.263
20	6.623	6.259	5.929	5.628	5.353	5.101	4.870	4.657	4.460	4.279
25	6.873	6.464	6.097	5.766	5.467	5.195	4.948	4.721	4.514	4.323
30	7.003	6.566	6.177	5.829	5.517	5.235	4.979	4.746	4.534	4.339
35	7.070	6.617	6.215	5.858	5.539	5.251	4.992	4.756	4.541	4.345
40	7.105	6.642	6.234	5.871	5.548	5.258	4.997	4.760	4.544	4.347
45	7.123	6.654	6.242	5.877	5.552	5.261	4.999	4.761	4.545	4.347
50	7.133	6.661	6.246	5.880	5.554	5.262	5.000	4.762	4.545	4.348

Note: The above present value factors are based on year-end interest calculations.

24%	25%	26%	27%	28%	29%	30%	35%	40%
.807	.800	.794	.787	.781	.775	.769	.741	.714
1.457	1.440	1.424	1.407	1.392	1.376	1.361	1.289	1.224
1.981	1.952	1.923	1.896	1.868	1.842	1.816	1.696	1.589
2.404	2.362	2.320	2.280	2.241	2.203	2.166	1.997	1.849
2.745	2.689	2.635	2.583	2.532	2.483	2.436	2.220	2.035
3.021	2.951	2.885	2.821	2.759	2.700	2.643	2.385	2.168
3.242	3.161	3.083	3.009	2.937	2.868	2.802	2.508	2.263
3.421	3.329	3.241	3.156	3.076	2.999	2.925	2.598	2.331
3.566	3.463	3.366	3.273	3.184	3.100	3.019	2.665	2.379
3.682	3.571	3.465	3.366	3.269	3.178	3.092	2.715	2.414
3.776	3.656	3.544	3.437	3.335	3.239	3.147	2.752	2.438
3.851	3.725	3.606	3.493	3.387	3.286	3.190	2.779	2.456
3.912	3.780	3.656	3.538	3.427	3.322	3.223	2.799	2.469
3.962	3.824	3.695	3.573	3.459	3.351	3.249	2.814	2.478
4.001	3.859	3.726	3.601	3.483	3.373	3.268	2.825	2.484
4.033	3.887	3.751	3.623	3.503	3.390	3.283	2.834	2.489
4.059	3.910	3.771	3.640	3.518	3.403	3.295	2.840	2.492
4.080	3.928	3.786	3.654	3.529	3.413	3.304	2.844	2.494
4.097	3.942	3.799	3.666	3.539	3.421	3.311	2.848	2.496
4.110	3.954	3.808	3.673	3.546	3.427	3.316	2.850	2.497
4.147	3.985	3.834	3.694	3.564	3.442	3.329	2.856	2.499
4.160	3.995	3.842	3.701	3.569	3.447	3.332	2.857	2.500
4.164	3.998	3.845	3.703	3.571	3.448	3.333	2.857	2.500
4.166	3.999	3.846	3.703	3.571	3.448	3.333	2.857	2.500
4.166	4.000	3.846	3.704	3.571	3.448	3.333	2.857	2.500
4.167	4.000	3.846	3.704	3.571	3.448	3.333	2.857	2.500

Note: The above present value factors are based on year-end interest calculations.

Appendix C
Glossary of terms

advance corporation tax	A part of the total corporation tax liability which is paid to the Inland Revenue at the time a dividend is paid to shareholders.
capital allowance	The Inland Revenue's equivalent of a company's depreciation charge. Allowances are granted on purchases of certain new assets and reduce taxable profits.
capital gearing	See *gearing*.
corporation tax	The tax levied on a limited company's profit. There is one basic rate (currently 52%) but a small company rate (of 40%) applies to companies earning low profits.
current cost accounting	A procedure for adjusting items in a company profit and loss account and balance sheet for the effects of inflation.
decision tree	A diagram depicting alternative courses of action as branches of a tree.

depreciation	A proportion of the original or current replacement cost of a fixed asset which is charged as an expense in a company profit and loss account.
discounted cash flow (DCF) yield	A measure of the true rate of profitability expected on a project. It represents the maximum rate of interest which could be paid on the diminishing capital balance of an investment.
dividend yield	The dividend per share expressed as a % of the current market price of the share.
equity	See *shareholders' funds*.
fixed assets	Land and buildings, plant and machinery, vehicles, furniture and office equipment used by the firm itself and not resold to customers.
gearing	The relationship of borrowed capital to owners' capital.
historic cost	The actual cost incurred at the time of purchase irrespective of the item's current value.
income tax	The tax levied on the income of employees and on the profits of self-employed persons.

inflation accounting	See *current cost accounting*.
life cycle cost	The total cost of owning and using a physical asset over its whole life, from its original design and manufacture to its eventual disposal.
mainstream tax	The balance of the corporation tax liability after the advance payments have been made.
mutually exclusive	Projects are said to be mutually exclusive when they compete against each other and only one alternative may be chosen.
net present value (NPV)	The total of all positive and negative cash flows on a project after they have been expressed in present value terms. A project is said to be viable when a positive net present value results from discounting at the company's required rate of return.
nominal return	The apparent rate of return on an investment calculated from inflated future cash flows.
opportunity cost	The value forgone from the next best use of the same resources.
payback	The number of years taken to recover the original sum invested.

present value	The equivalent value now of a sum of money receivable in a later year.
probability factor	The likelihood of occurrence of a particular event represented by a number ranging from 0 to 1.0. A probability factor of 0 implies no chance of the event occurring whilst a factor of 1.0 depicts the certainty of it happening.
profitability index	A means of ranking investments in order of attractiveness when appraised by the net present value method. The index number is calculated by dividing the net present value inflows by the net present value outflows.
real return	The nominal rate of return on an investment less the rate of inflation.
rights issue	An invitation to existing shareholders to subscribe for new shares when a company requires further capital.
risk premium	The rate by which the basic cost of capital is increased to allow for the expected risk on an investment.

sensitivity analysis	A process to discover the responsiveness of the profitability of an investment to variations in individual items making up the cash flows.
shareholders' funds	The total amount of shareholders' investment in the company comprising both issued share capital, retained profits and other reserves. It is also equal to the value of all the company's assets after deducting all debts owing to outside parties.
stock relief	A tax allowance for the effects of inflation on the value of a company's stocks and work-in-progress during the year.
terotechnology	A combination of management, financial, engineering and other practices applied to physical assets in pursuit of economic life cycle costs.
working capital	That part of a firm's total capital which is tied up in stocks, work-in-progress and granting credit to customers. It is equal to the total value of all stocks, customers' debts and cash less the amount owing to suppliers.

Index